INTENTIONAL DISCIPLE

A 31-Day Devotional
Discovering Your New Identity in Christ

Sherry Dale

WESTBOW
P R E S S®
A DIVISION OF THOMAS NELSON
& ZONDERVAN

WestBow Press books may be ordered through booksellers or by contacting:

WestBow Press
A Division of Thomas Nelson & Zondervan
1663 Liberty Drive
Bloomington, IN 47403
www.westbowpress.com
844-714-3454

ISBN: 978-1-6642-0233-7 (sc)
ISBN: 978-1-6642-0234-4 (e)

Library of Congress Control Number: 2020915478

Print information available on the last page.

WestBow Press rev. date: 09/10/2020

Dedication

I dedicate this book to my husband Jack. Thank you for your perpetual joy that wakes me with a smile every day, for your unending love that seems to never end no matter what comes our way and your constant encouragement cheering me from every sideline. You inspire me to be the best version of myself for Jesus. There is no one else that I would rather grow up and grow old with than you.

Acknowledgement

First, I would like to thank our Heavenly Father. My highest honor is to share Your love with the world. May any and all glory be Yours.

I would especially like to thank Becky Getz for her many hours of kind, editing feedback and to Laura Taliaferro, who kept me accountable to never stop this project. Everyone should be blessed to have an amazing cheerleader like you.

And to all of the encouraging friends who have helped bring this book to life, thank you. What a blessing to sit at the feet of Jesus and study His Word with you, to carry one another's prayers to His throne and to see His face revealed in yours. You each are a gift to me.

Finally, with deepest appreciation, I especially would like to thank my darling daughter Summer for her expert advice and encouragement throughout this project. Thank you for being the first set of eyes to read and reread so many scribbled pages and for always hearing what I was trying to say. And to my precious son Jackson who I can always count on to motivate and remind me to fully share what God speaks. Thank you both for always believing in me. I love you both more than life will show.

Contents

Foreword

Wow! A masterpiece! I have never seen so much rich, in depth content, saturated with Scripture, contained in a one month devotional. Yet it is simple, understandable, and practical! This book is "on point", no fluff! It will challenge you to GROW!

I have known Sherry since she married Jack, decades ago. Jack interned at our ministry and we later served together on staff. I was their Sunday School teacher when their daughter Summer was young. Sherry is the real deal! Her faith is unwavering! Her heart is sold out to Jesus! Combine that with her experience as a wife, mom, and many years as a middle school teacher, and you understand how God so masterfully used her to chronicle these essential truths of the faith.

It will challenge you to go deep, yet in very practical terms. I believe this book is so anointed because Sherry lives it …day in and day out, in the trenches of life. Sherry is a woman of God (WOG), and her desire is to challenge you to become a woman or man of God (WOG, MOG) …or if you are a young person, a YWOG or YMOG.

I have never met a single person that became a godly Christ follower by accident. You purpose to. It is your choice! As this book states often, "it must be intentional" if you desire to be His image bearer!

I often ask people about their spiritual journey and how they view their current spiritual growth curve. A common response is, "Well, right now, I have kind of plateaued, not really growing, but not necessarily falling away either." There is a serious problem with that answer. It's impossible! You do not spiritually plateau. Just like any plant life or other living thing, you are either growing or dying —no plateau! Jesus said, *"there is no neutral ground ...if you're not helping, you're making things worse."* (Mt. 12:30 MSG)

This devotional tool will help get you growing again and chasing after your Savior like never before. I once heard it said, "The Christian life is either a whole lot more than I am experiencing or a whole lot less than it is cracked up to be." I was the former and had to intentionally choose to dig into God's Word daily, and *then* the "experience" was off the charts! Everyone around me could see the radical difference because it was obvious that I had "been with Jesus."

You will always find time for what is most important to you! We all worship something. If Jesus really is important to you, you will find time for Him daily. I can think of no better way to jumpstart your walk than this guide of non-negotiables of the faith that will help you dig into the Scriptures.

A verse that continually came to mind as I was using this devotional is when Paul said, *"All I want to know is Christ"* (Phil. 3:10 CEV) *"My goal is to Know Him"* (Phil. 3:10 HCSB). My favorite version is the Amplified Bible: *For my determined purpose is that I may know Him that I may progressively become more deeply and intimately acquainted with Him, perceiving and recognizing and understanding the wonders of His Person more strongly and more clearly... to be continually transformed in spirit into His likeness...*

Paul pretty much sums up this book, ***"For my determined purpose is that I may know Him!"***

As Sherry often admits throughout these devotional writings, it is not always easy and it requires effort. Heb. 12:11 (MSG) says: *At the time, discipline isn't much fun. It always feels like it's going against the grain. Later, of course, it pays off handsomely, for it's the well-trained who find themselves mature in their relationship with God.*

Once you get into a rhythm of meeting daily with God, it will likely become a pattern for life. As scripture begins to saturate your mind you will experience an unexplainable presence of God on your life. You will have a new awareness of Him working through you at every turn …growing you as He uses you as a witness to encourage others.

One of the great scriptural truths is that obedience brings about the blessing and favor of God. My prayer for you is that you approach this more teachable and hungry than ever (absorb, soak up), and just watch in wonder as He pours out His favor on your life!

My recommendation on how to use this tool: In the first year, you will want to use this devotional more than one month! It is that rich! And it will take more than once to fully digest its treasures. It did for me. And after that, I think you will want to go through it at least one month each year as a refresher course in the basic essentials of the faith.

Feast and enjoy!
Billy Beacham
Director of Student Discipleship Ministries and one of the founders of "See You at the Pole" global student prayer movement.

Preface

Who would have thought that a tiny devotional book could change a life? But it did. My hope is that this one will eternally bless someone else. Author Greta Rey's *Good Morning, Lord* was the vehicle God used that eventually led me straight to Him. As an only child of divorce, my Heavenly Father became the face I longed to see each morning. By the time I was 12 years of age, I actually understood what Jesus died for, who Jesus died for. And I realized it was me.

With a cup of hot coffee in one hand and my beloved Bible in the other, my favorite wake-up call is still the moment the sun sings, "Good morning, Lord" to the world. As the sacred crescendo rises, I snuggle into a quiet reading spot to discover what God will say to me each day. Soon, I recognize His voice. I see His glorious face as His Word comes alive and off the page as it is born again in me. As time passes, I realize that I must seek Him or I will not see Him. God can be easy to miss if you are not looking for Him. We must be intentional.

For me, I recognize God's face and feel most loved by Him when I see the wonderful family that He has graced me with. Beyond salvation, my greatest blessing on earth was when He led me to Jack, the love of my life. After graduation, we married, and, three years later God overwhelmed me with His love as we welcomed our first child into the world. As her name suggests, Summer Ainsley has always been a "refreshing bringer of the Word of life." Her love of God's creation decorates her beautiful, creative spirit. Sharing Bible stories with her was always a highlight for me as we learned together. Many I heard for the first time as we read them together aloud. The Holy Spirit taught me as I taught her.

Six years later, our adorable son, Jackson, was born. With a contagious smile that touched the hearts of everyone he came in contact with, his busy days were filled with play and joyful delight. These two were best buddies and now it was Summer who was first in line to read those Bible stories aloud to him. Jack and I had committed to living our faith in front of them as we did our best to demonstrate the love of Jesus to them. It was Jackson's last official summer before leaving for his freshman year of college when my soul started slightly panicking. What if being raised in a Christian home was not enough? What if someone asks him a question about his faith and we have not prepared him well enough? What if? What if? All these doubts began flooding into my concerned mind. Don't get me wrong, God had graced us with a son that we could not be prouder of, but letting go has not always been one of my strong points. It was then that the Holy Spirit gently spoke to me and said, "Sherry, you have now."

It was then that God's peace poured over my anxious heart. I asked my six-foot-tall son to join me on the floor and to please bring his Bible. "Daddy and I will not always be with you but God will. He has provided every answer to your every question, right here," I said as I put my hand on his Bible. "I have peace in knowing that Jesus is your Lord and Savior and nothing could make your dad and I more thankful. But you are about to enter a season where you will no longer be living by our rules out of obedience. You will be walking out your own relationship with God. You will be making your own decisions in a world that may not always be kind. May I walk with you through some topics of Scripture and show you what I mean? Just in case you need them along the way." He said yes, and our quest began.

Friend, that was the exact moment that the manuscript you hold in your hands was first conceived. Father God carried me through nine years of labor before that seed, planted within my heart, was fully mature enough to be birthed. I could not write about something I had not first lived, so as life was experienced, the Holy Spirit had me journal. It was for you.

My hope is that these pages will support holy habits in you. Let them strengthen your new journey of grace and inspire your confidence for this walk of a lifetime.

Introduction

Let's face it, dear friends: The Word of God has not diminished in beauty since our Heavenly Father first whispered life into the faithful ones He instructed to record His voice. Though Jesus Christ, the Word become flesh, has not changed, Christians most certainly have. Most people have few arguments regarding the sacrificial and holy life of Jesus Christ, yet His disciples on earth are not always that convincing. It is not typically Jesus that humanity disagrees with; rather, it is His followers that are frankly found not to be worth following.

Many in the world who really want to walk like Jesus are frustrated because they simply cannot seem to find Him in the people who claim to follow Him. Think about it: so many folks calling themselves believers today walk nothing like our Jesus in the Bible. How confusing is that? Therefore, this is emerging into quite a confused generation of Christendom. When truth is too quiet, the voice of deception begins sounding pretty loud—so loud, in fact, that lies begin masking the face of truth. Inevitably, people start believing those loud lies and false doctrine results. Without delay, now is the time for all believers to stand up, shine the light on the darkness, and encourage followers of Christ and not-yet-followers to truly follow Christ! I am in no way suggesting that I have spiritually arrived; the Lord knows that I am far from being perfect. If I was, I would not need Him so. However, one thing that I am 100 percent certain of is that every answer to every one of life's questions can be found in God's Holy Word.

As you have taken your first step toward preparing for eternity, from this day forward you will not just get older but you will grow older. This kind of spiritual growth is called discipleship. Growing into a mature disciple not only takes time but it takes time alone with Him. And no one can do that for you. Beyond having your own personal Bible in a translation that speaks to your understanding, I suggest for each believer—new and old—to begin purposefully reading it every day. A wonderful place to begin is the book of John, which is an intense introduction into the life of Jesus and His incredible love for us.

Together, for the next 31 days, we will create a holy habit of putting God first in time alone with Him. The tool you hold in your hands will support your passion for a deeper relationship with Jesus and guide you through various topics within the Bible. By faithfully reading His Word daily and learning biblical principles, you will love your Savior even more deeply.

My hope is to encourage your journey and inspire confidence in your new relationship as an intentional disciple. After all, these pages are only one traveler's journey of grace. And at the end of every day, my feet still need a good washing. The One and only One who is consistently worth following is Jesus.

DAY 1

What Are Your Intentions?

"I will put My Spirit within you and cause you to walk in My statutes, and you will be careful to observe My ordinances."

Ezekiel 36:27 (NASB)

True disciples do not just happen. They are intentionally made. Just as students must discipline themselves to learn from their teacher's words, so disciples of Christ are trained to be disciples by the words of Christ. They must be intentional. In other words, they are to be "deliberate, intended, purposeful or done by intention," as *Merriam-Webster* defines. By purposefully loving God and reading His Word daily, disciplined habits strengthen our commitment.

Let the following scenario paint a picture to illustrate this point. Imagine that we are viewing a classic vintage movie entitled "Intentions." We may have encountered the climactic scene where a nervous young boy wants to date a man's daughter. The father eventually decides to ask the young man the dreaded question: "Exactly what are your intentions, son?" This is followed by Dad's stern eyes peering over his bifocals. At this point, after the fearful young fellow stops shaking, he replies with the assurance of the hopeful possibility of a relational commitment, "I would like to discover if we could have a future together, sir." Hopefully, this is the truth, but whether the future groom means it or not, he feels compelled to say these words. In contrast, if those words were not

1

honest, he could have uttered out of his mouth what his mind was actually thinking. This would definitely have gotten him nowhere but trouble. If we could read his mind, and his plan was not positive, something else may have been uttered: "Uh, sir, I just want to use your daughter for my own selfish gain. After all, it is all about me. So when this relationship is no longer convenient, and she is no longer desired, I will just say goodbye. Thus, returning the shattered pieces of her broken heart back to you."

Though painfully true, his motives would definitely have gone unrewarded.

Okay, so maybe that scenario is a bit harsh to begin a book entitled *Intentional Disciple*, but unfortunately this kind of self-focused dating has crept its way into the church today. Selfishness continues to court sinful behavior when the caution of discernment goes unexercised. This happens spiritually in the lives of many new believers, unfortunately, when commitment seems vague.

Engagement with the one you love should not be a self-focused relationship but rather one that is loved-one focused. The commitment level must be deep if it is to last. I would like to present the same question as the pervasive father in the previous scene.

What exactly are your intentions, my friend? Have you chosen to spiritually "date" Jesus, or are you sincerely "engaged" with Him?

In other words, "Why are you a Christian"?

My prayer is that, at the precious moment when you asked Jesus Christ into your heart to be your Savior, the words uttered from your lips were serious and sincere. In reality, only God knows the ultimate intentions of all of our hearts and the truth behind our words to Him. However, if saying a prayer was as meaningful as "a shotgun wedding with all eyes on you" or as selfish as "it may be good for business," then I ask you to take a moment of prayerful consideration regarding the level of your commitment to the Heavenly Father.

This relationship is for all eternity, not for a day or a week, but forever. "For better or for worse, for richer or for poorer, in sickness and in health" may be words that echo during wedding ceremonies, but they can definitely apply here. This is an eternal love. Once we have said, "Yes, I do" and accepted the Father's invitation, then we are expected to be intentional! Only God knows, but if we are not intentional about our relationship, are we even genuinely committed enough to be called a Christian at all?

My hope is that the greatest desire of our hearts will be *Jesus Christ*, so we can say with Isaiah, "Yes, Lord, walking in the way of your laws, we wait for You; Your name and renown are the desire of our hearts" (Isaiah 26:8, NIV).

JOURNAL your memory of when you personally chose to say, "Yes" to Christ.

_____

_____

_____

_____

_____

_____

_____

_____

_____

_____

_____

_____

_____

_____

_____

_____

_____

If this proposal is new to you, tomorrow was written with you in mind. You need not wait. Read on, my friend.

DAY 2

A Disciple by Invitation

"Everyone who calls on the name of the Lord will be saved."

Romans 10:13 (NIV)

Life's distractions prevent many of us from walking focused with intention. Taking God at His Word to strengthen eternal devotion to Him takes a pure and purposeful step-by-step determination. The acceptance of God's proposal of His love through Jesus will make a difference in the rest of our lives.

You see, this life we each live in this world is not all there is. God created us to live with Him for eternity. Forever. We were made for His purposes and not only ours alone. The interesting thing to me is that our life on earth is actually our time of preparation for this eternity—the eternity that we spend worshipping Him.

The Heavenly Father desires for all of the world to live with Him forever in heaven. Though all have generously been invited to come, not everyone chooses to say yes to accept His invitation. Imagine a neighbor opening their mailbox and finding that they had been invited to a party that would be held at another location in the future. They now have a choice. To go or not to go. To respond, an RSVP of yes or no would be in order.

To parallel this analogy with a spiritual application, that mailbox on earth would represent our heart spiritually. Delivered especially to you by the spiritual messenger known as the Holy Spirit of God, the invitation would depict the request of one's presence for the future heavenly celebration.

One catch, though: each of us must die physically on earth before arriving in heaven. This makes this love letter time-sensitive, so it is critical that we each personally RSVP while still living on this earth. I do not mean to oversimplify the gravity of this decision. I only wish to impart the true significance of this acceptance being timely.

And honestly, friends, we must seriously realize that this divine party in heaven is not dependent on whether you or I say yes or no. It will happen either way. You or I just will or will not be there. For it is not our response that determines whether the future celebration takes place; rather, it is a question of whether or not we will be attending. The response to this invitation is truly an eternal matter of life or death. But the choice remains ours.

Every last one of us actually deserves eternal death, according to Romans 3:23, for "all [of us] have sinned and fallen short of the glory of God." Three chapters later, Romans 6:23 continues in identifying that "the wages of sin is death." In other words, not one of us can be good enough to enter heaven on our own. But praise our holy yet merciful God, our salvation is not based on the works that we do but on our acceptance of His loving invitation.

All expenses have so graciously been paid by Jesus in His death on the cross. It is not what we do for Him but what He has done for us that determines whether we enter. It is not our sin that prevents us from entering heaven. It is our rejection of His payment for our sin.

Let's focus deeper on the words of Romans 6:23. It begins with the wages, or payment, of our sin being eternal separation known as death. In contrast, it goes on to say that "the free gift of God is eternal life in Christ Jesus our Lord." This gift of grace is free! Grace has been anonymously defined as "God's Riches At Christ's Expense." True.

No matter how it is defined, the grace God has so lavishly poured out upon us is so undeserved, which makes me love Him more. God demonstrated this great love for us with the cross. But He did not make us wait until we were good enough either. No! Instead, "while we were yet sinners, Christ died for us" (Romans 5:8, NASB). Oh, I am so thankful for the relentless love of God!

God is Love and has always loved us. 1 John 4:19 states that God first loved us, even when we did not even know Him. Each and every one of us has been invited to this heavenly celebration. Though undeserving, not one of us has been left off of the guest list. However, God still gives us the choice to respond.

If you have not already responded to God's loving invitation, you can even now. Please pray with me, from your heart, the following:

God, I know that I need You. I admit that I have sinned. Please forgive me. Thank you for loving me, God. I want to accept Jesus as my Savior. I say "yes" to your invitation. I do believe that Jesus died for me and I now want to live for Him, to live for You. Come into my heart, Jesus, to be the Lord of my every decision for I am now eternally Yours. Please help me to live a life that appreciates and follows You all the way home. It is in Jesus' name that I pray. Amen.

The angels in heaven are rejoicing over your decision. Please know that I, too, am celebrating in my heart for you, dear friend. Together as we eagerly wait, may we intentionally share God's love with those in the world who have not yet heard that they, too, have been invited.

JOURNAL a heart-felt thank you note to God for His invitation of love.

_____

_____

_____

_____

_____

_____

_____

_____

_____

_____

_____

_____

_____

_____

_____

_____

_____

_____

_____

_____

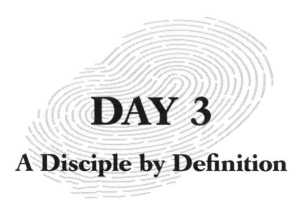

DAY 3

A Disciple by Definition

"Therefore go and make disciples of all nations, baptizing them in the name of the Father and of the Son and of the Holy Spirit, and teaching them to obey everything I have commanded you. And surely I am with you always, to the very end of the age."

Matthew 28:19-20 (NIV)

The commitment of following Jesus Christ with all of our heart is evidenced in what I call being an *intentional disciple*. In chapter 28 of the Gospel of Matthew, while Jesus was still on the earth speaking to His followers, He purposefully left sacred directions for when He would no longer be with them in the flesh. He also reassured them that they would not be alone in this world and that His presence would forever be with them. These comforting instructions are referred to as the *Great Commission*.

He directed His followers, otherwise known as disciples, to actually go and to make more disciples. So, what is a disciple? A disciple is simply a learner, a student, a pupil, a disciplined follower, or one who sits at the feet of the teacher for the purpose of being taught. So, in order for a person to be a disciple, there always must first be a teacher who teaches by example so the student can follow. Our teacher is Jesus Christ and He left us an instruction manual called the Bible that includes examples of how He lived these teachings out in the flesh while He lived on earth. God also has given us His Spirit to live within us and to help us to understand these teachings, as it is written in John 14:26.

Once we have made the decision to follow Christ, choosing to remain the same is not an option. Though it is a process, the time to begin learning to walk begins immediately after your invitation has been accepted. Walking involves action, and action always requires movement. And, though it may feel uncomfortable at first, this new way of walking will soon become second nature to you as you grow because this new you is exactly who God created you to be all along.

"So, who are you following?" The answer can be found with one more poignant question, "Who do you walk like?" *The fact is a follower of Christ walks like Christ.*

We learn to follow Jesus Christ by listening to God's voice as we read His holy words in the Bible. Because we are His pupil, the Lord should be the companion we most intimately spend time with daily. As a disciple of Jesus Christ, we learn to walk one step at a time in the right direction.

Being personally guided by the Holy Spirit in our own individual hearts is essential to drawing close in our intimacy with Him. I am not implying that we cannot reap from other students in life's classroom. However, if we are not careful, laziness can lead us to rely on the wisdom that God has given other believers without ever spending time with Him alone.

To illustrate this truth, let's compare a piece of fresh fruit to processed fruit juice. Both are tasty but fresh fruit always gives fuller, richer health benefits that endure. Processed foods lack dense nutritional value though they can be a quick sweetness for the moment. Honestly, there may be some days when fast little fruit snacks are the very best thing we have available, but I encourage you to let that be the exception and not the rule. In order for us to grow physically healthy, we must eat physically healthy. The same is true spiritually. We will grow more fruit of the Spirit if we allow God to teach through the process of spiritual depth and not just let the processed end result become a focus. Or, as I have heard it said, "the deeper the root, the bigger the fruit!"

Intentionally sitting at the feet of your teacher will train and equip your walk more faithfully. There is no substitute for this. We may share the road with other trusted believers but we are ultimately a follower of Christ, not another person. No one else's quiet time can be compared to your own personal time of devotion spent alone with God, the love of your life.

I repeat; never underestimate the value of your own personal time spent with your God. Remember, as much as we love the Word of God, we also must spend time loving the *God of the Word*. No one else can do that for you.

JOURNAL your commitment to be intentional about spending time with God daily, knowing that time and commitment go hand in hand with love.

_____

_____

_____

_____

_____

_____

_____

_____

_____

_____

_____

_____

_____

_____

_____

_____

_____

_____

DAY 4

Being a Disciple Makes a Difference

"We are in this world but not of this world."

John 15:19 (NIV)

Jesus reminds His disciples in both John 15:19 and 17:14 that "We are in this world but not of this world." Though we may still be physically in this world, we are spiritually of the kingdom of God once Jesus Christ has taken up residence within us. Now that Jesus has been invited into our hearts, He begins to spiritually make Himself at home. If you are like me, that may also involve a lot of house cleaning.

As He dwells and lives with us, our home just cannot run the same as it did before Jesus was living there. Robert Boyd Munger illustrates this process flawlessly in one of my favorite classic books entitled *My Heart-Christ's Home*. As the Spirit of God journeys into each room of his heart, Munger helps the reader to identify what needs to be removed, not only in his life but also in ours. Though I have read this more times than I can count, the Lord uses it to richly speak to me on each occasion.

With Jesus living inside of us, we soon begin to look differently inside and out. (However, on the outside, if we had freckles and brown hair before our salvation, we do still have freckles and brown hair after we pray.) We don't look different but we *look* different. The way we see things may change. Eventually, some of the people, places, or things that were acceptable in the past to hang around may now begin feeling wrong, like they just don't fit you anymore. That is because you are absolutely right. You *are* different! You are out-of-this-world different because you are *not of this world*.

The one who follows Jesus Christ and the one who is led astray by the ways of the world are walking in two completely different directions. Following Christ is a new and living way, and every spiritual student disciplines himself or herself to walk in this way even when the climb is hard.

As pupils of Jesus, we are no longer to even try to follow and become like the world and its world system; instead, we are to practice holiness. As we practice and practice and practice holiness, we will learn holiness. There *should* be a definitive difference in the life actions of an intentional disciple. This distinction was clarified in the Old Testament as the Lord spoke to Aaron, the priest, recorded in Leviticus 10:10: "Put difference between holy and unholy, and between unclean and clean." Sobering. Can it get any clearer than that? Holiness is that difference.

Holiness is the distinguishing feature for a child of God to be identified. The Holy Spirit that lives inside of us is actually the Spirit of the holiness of God. "Since we have these promises, dear friends, let us purify ourselves from everything that contaminates body and spirit, perfecting holiness out of reverence for God" (2 Corinthians 7:1, NIV). As disciples of Christ, we are to purposefully come out from among those things of the world that do not represent Jesus.

This may also involve relationships. No longer allowing the world to lead you astray means that we are more careful in who we allow to have the strongest impact over us. 1 John 2:15-17 reminds us that if anyone loves the world more than they love God the Father, they are not following God's will. So, friend, be careful with whom you allow to be your greatest influence. By our continual association with the world, it may become easy to resemble a worldly person.

Before we know it, worldly living dangerously creeps in and becomes the pattern we desire to be fashioned by.

1 Corinthians 15:33 reminds us that "bad company corrupts good morals." This scripture came to life recently at my school. As a middle school health teacher for the past seventeen years, I attempt to encourage my young teens to daily make positive friend choices. This day was no exception. As we were discussing the value of positive influences, one of my seventh grade students boldly spoke up and said, "My momma always says, 'You are the company you keep.'" I responded, "Smart momma." I carried this concept a step further by demonstrating that it is like trying to put strawberries and onions in the same plastic Ziploc bag and hoping that they both taste good. It just does not happen. Spiritually, the same principle can be applied. We soon become like those we spend a lot of time with.

What about those friends who have not chosen to accept God's invitation yet? I encourage you to diligently pray for them. None of us are better than another; rather, we have just been forgiven. Those who don't know this must be shown this. So keep praying for their hearts to be open to the acceptance of God's love and forgiveness. They will see Jesus in your changed life as you live out your testimony of His grace without compromise. You may even be the very one God uses to deliver the good news to them.

In conclusion, choose well who you spend the most time with and value those righteous influencers that the Lord sends your way. As believers in Christ, our closest associations should be those who love the Word of God. Treasure them. Align with Psalm 119:63, so that we may also say, "I am a companion of all those who fear You, and of those who keep Your precepts."

JOURNAL your desire to make Jesus more at home in your heart by asking the Holy Spirit if there is anyone or anything that you need His help to remove. Courageously ask Him now.

_____

_____

_____

_____

_____

_____

_____

_____

_____

_____

_____

_____

_____

_____

_____

_____

_____

_____

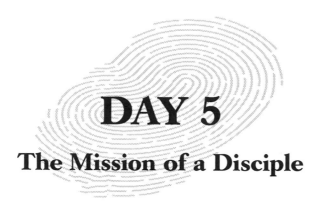

DAY 5

The Mission of a Disciple

"Jesus said to them again, 'Peace be with you; as
the Father has sent me, I also send you.'"

John 20:21 (NASB)

As our love for Jesus Christ deepens, we will be satisfied with no less than giving Him our best. This faithful response requires faithful obedience as His representative. He is now sending us out on a mission as well. "Peace to you; as the Father has sent Me, I also send you [as My representatives]" (John 20:21, AMP).

In chapter 28 of the Gospel of Matthew, we read the last words that Jesus spoke to His followers: "Go and make disciples of all nations, baptizing them in the name of the Father and of the Son and of the Holy Spirit, and teaching them to obey everything I have commanded you" (Matthew 28:19, NIV).

Without a doubt, every word spoken by the Son of God is life-changing, but these were His final words before He was crucified. This statement would be considered His last will and testament, just like when someone is about to die and they leave the family a will declaring their final wishes. Though spoken almost 2,000 years ago, these instructions of Jesus continue to be applicable for all of His followers, both past and present. We are not exempt, and we must take these words seriously.

Jesus not only gave His followers instructions for the future, but

He also infused these commands with the authority of His name to enforce them. We can take tremendous comfort in Matthew 28:20 and John 20:21, that His Holy Spirit would remain with His followers as He was living in them. He would be with them always. Intentional disciple, this promise is ours as well. You can walk out your calling with boldness and confident assurance knowing that He is with you and you will never be alone again. This assurance is also found in Deuteronomy 31:6: "Be strong and courageous. Do not be afraid or terrified because of them, for the Lord your God goes with you; he will never leave you nor forsake you" (NIV).

Jesus is the Holy Word of God lived out. He became flesh and dwelt among us, as recorded in John 1:14. He has shown us how to live out God's will page after page within the Bible. The written Word of God is our gift of God's promise to us in writing. He has given us the Holy Spirit of God to live within us, empowering us to follow His example in walking out the Word in our generation. His indwelling presence is the eternal gift of the Holy Spirit of God sent to every disciple.

During a weekly radio broadcast that I caught one day on my drive home, Pastor Alistair Begg of Cleveland's Parkside Church, proclaimed a powerful statement reinforcing the value of listening to the voice of God. I pulled the car over and quickly captured as best I could the following. "The fact is that what God has to say to us is infinitely more significant than what we have to say to Him... if that were not the case, there'd be no reason for Him to have given us a Bible, no reason for Him to have given us the Holy Spirit to help us understand the Bible and no reason for Him to have sent His Son which was of course the incarnate Word."

How powerful! We must be determined to listen well to His voice that we may carry His Word within our hearts, for only then do we carry Him. This is our true mission after all. It is the Jesus Christ within us that is this world's only hope. They are desperately seeking Him. So let's go. We've got a story to tell: His!

JOURNAL your commitment to Jesus' instructions by inserting your name.

_____, "go and make disciples of all nations, baptizing them in the name of the Father and of the Son and of the Holy Spirit, and teaching them to obey everything I have commanded you" (Matthew 28:19, NIV).

Pray and ask God to highlight ways that the Great Commission can be implemented in your life.

_____

_____

_____

_____

_____

_____

_____

_____

_____

_____

_____

_____

_____

_____

_____

_____

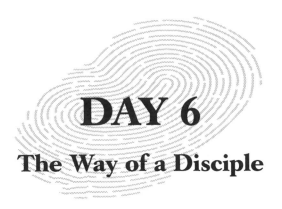

DAY 6

The Way of a Disciple

"Whoever claims to live in him must walk as Jesus did."

1 John 2:6 (NIV)

As the earthly ministry of Jesus was drawing to a close, I so appreciate how He continually prepared His beloved disciples for what was about to happen. Though they did not completely understand everything that He was saying, it would soon be unveiled before their eyes as He chose to reveal it.

As they continued to pursue a deeper understanding of the Living Word walking in their midst, they recognized that Jesus Christ was the very Messiah that generations had patiently waited for. The Anointed One was now literally walking in their midst, and He was the only one worth walking with.

The disciples knew that Jesus was the way, the truth, and the life, as recorded in John 14:6. His walk was not only a directional path for life's journey, He was the WAY. He was not only speaking truth, He was the TRUTH. Jesus not only had miraculous signs of life accompanying His ministry, He was LIFE and life everlasting.

Throughout the land, those who were following Him began walking like Him, talking like Him, and acting like Him. As they assembled together in gatherings, people met together in homes and these homes became churches. One of these churches was in Antioch.

In Acts 11:26, these Antioch followers were first referred to as Christians. This word "Christian" implied a reversal of a walk that was so evident to the onlookers that the direction of their life-walk had literally changed. Disciples were called "Christians" because they followed Jesus Christ's Way, His way of walking, His way of talking. They intentionally followed His way of life with purpose.

A couple of years ago, as I researched the actual Greek definition of the word "Christian," I found that the word translated "Christian" literally means "a follower of Christ." Today, a person may call themselves a Christian, but further research indicated that this was not the case in A.D. 33. Originally, the term was not one used by people who called themselves a follower of Christ. In other words, the word "Christian" was not a term that the followers of Christ gave *to themselves;* rather, it was a term that *others* called them! "But why?"

Because their life walk was so convincing of a drastic change in direction, people associated this new walk with that of Jesus. Thus, they began calling them "Christians" behind their backs because the evidence was so convincing. It took courage to stand up and walk like Him. We must be careful not to freely call ourselves Christians if the proof is lacking. This way of walking looked so much like the way that Jesus modeled that this movement of following Jesus was actually referred to as "the Way" in Acts 9:2. May we step up to the life-walk that God intended and have others call us a "Christian" simply by the evidence of the way we are walking.

JOURNAL your desire to wholeheartedly follow the way of Jesus Christ so that "Christian" is what others are calling you.

_____

_____

_____

_____

_____

_____

_____

_____

_____

_____

_____

_____

_____

_____

_____

_____

_____

_____

_____

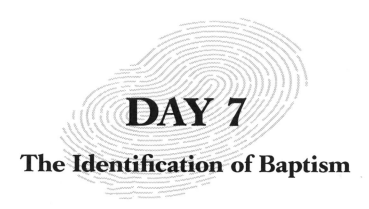

DAY 7

The Identification of Baptism

"If you love me, you will obey what I command."

John 14:15 (NIV)

From the time that God created the heavens and the earth, He has desired a relationship with the ones His hands have made. Our Creator not only spoke the world into existence, but He also spoke His Word miraculously into flesh to live on the very earth He made, states John 1:14. This Living Word is Jesus, and the reason He chose to dwell with us was to demonstrate how we must live. "I have set an example that you should do as I have done for you," says John 13:15 (NIV).

As disciples of Jesus Christ, we are to follow the example of Jesus out of obedience and out of our overwhelming love for Him. "If you love me, you will obey what I command" (John 14:15, NIV). Once we learn His Word and choose to obey His commands, we then give evidence of our love by our actions.

Once we have said yes to Love's voice when He calls, we declare it publicly. As evidence that we have accepted the message of Jesus Christ as our Savior and Lord and that we are not ashamed to be identified with Him, a disciple follows the Lord into the water of baptism. We find this example in Acts 2:14: "Those who accepted his message were baptized" (NIV).

We also are to be baptized because we are following the example given to us by Jesus Christ Himself, as recorded in Matthew 3:13-17 (NIV):

> Then Jesus came from Galilee to the Jordan to be baptized by John. But John tried to deter him, saying, "I need to be baptized by you, and do you come to me?" Jesus replied, "Let it be so now; it is proper for us to do this to fulfill all righteousness." Then John consented. As soon as Jesus was baptized, he went up out of the water. At that moment heaven was opened, and he saw the Spirit of God descending like a dove and lighting on him. And a voice from heaven said, "This is my Son, whom I love; with him I am well pleased."

What a beautiful picture of submission this was both for John the Baptist and for the very Son of God. Jesus faithfully demonstrated the fulfillment of God's plan for us. Because Jesus was perfect, He did not sin so it was not for His sin that He was baptized, but it was for our sin that He set an example for us to follow.

Baptism identifies us with the death, burial, and resurrection of Jesus Christ. As we identify with His death, we accept the gift of Jesus Himself being crucified, suffering an agonizing death upon the cross for us. We, too, intentionally put to death our spiritually old selves. This visual action of baptism is spiritually symbolic. It represents our intent to crucify the flesh and its deeds as represented by our submission as we approach the water. By giving all that we are to God, we confirm that we are willing to die to our self in humility and make God's will our new priority. We choose to daily nail the desires of our old self to the cross, as the apostle Paul writes to the church in Galatia: "I have been crucified with Christ and I no longer live, but Christ lives in me. The life I now live in the body, I live by faith in the Son of God, who loved me and gave himself for me" (Galatians 2:20, NIV).

We identify with His burial when we go under the water and are covered by the water. As believers are immersed into the waters of baptism, note that they are not bowing forward as one in control; rather, they are physically demonstrating their trust in God by falling back by faith as if to say that they are leaning on Him as they surrender to His way. Our old life has died with Him as we identify ourselves with Jesus' death. Having been buried with Him, we trust that our old life and its deeds are now put to death. As we are being submerged under the water, we accept His burial beneath the earth as we are covered not just by physical water but spiritually in His blood.

We also identify with His resurrection as we are raised out of the water of baptism. Just as Jesus was resurrected by the power of God from the grave, we are raised for His purpose to walk on this earth in the new and living way that Jesus Himself demonstrated. As we identify with Christ, we lay our lives down and begin living for Him. Our resurrected life is evidence to the world that Christ is alive, and now He is alive in you!

JOURNAL your own baptism experience. If your story has not yet been written, I encourage you to take this public step of obedience soon.

_____

_____

_____

_____

_____

_____

_____

_____

_____

_____

_____

_____

_____

_____

_____

_____

_____

_____

_____

DAY 8

The Walk of Baptism

"And that water is a picture of baptism, which now saves you, not by removing dirt from your body, but as a response to God from a clean conscience. It is effective because of the resurrection of Jesus Christ."

1 Peter 3:20-22 (NLT)

In the previous devotion, we learned that being baptized in water is a spiritual cleansing and purification from our old lives to a new walk. Stepping out of the baptistery and into the world, each disciple of Jesus Christ immediately begins to boldly demonstrate the truth to the mission field of earth. Our baptism serves as an inauguration into public ministry just as it did with Jesus.

In Matthew 28:19, the word "baptize" in the original Greek has several meanings. One is "to be fully wet and immersed." I visually equate this with birth. Even in the natural, a baby within its mother's womb is fully immersed in fluid, up until the water breaks. When it does, all who are publically present are thrilled to celebrate this new life. And so it is with baptism. This gives a whole new meaning to "born again," doesn't it?

When disciples of Jesus Christ are baptized, the beautiful body of Christ comes together as a unified spiritual family to welcome and celebrate. This is one reason that it is so important to get involved with a strong, biblically-based church. Those who are older in their spiritual relationship with God act as prayerful witnesses at this baptismal ceremony. The power of God lived out in their hearts will be the hands and feet of Jesus whenever needed.

Just as an infant must develop and grow, so we too spiritually grow up. But we all need help. Realize that there may be some falls along the way, but keep holding those more mature hands of accountability. They will help younger disciples learn how to walk this new life out as they should. A physical baby is not born in the world and then isolated to discover how survival of the fittest is played out. No, the baby is cared for and nurtured as he or she is fed until it can feed itself, cleaned until he or she learns to remove its own waste, and accepted in love as one of the family. We all know that learning how to walk takes time in the physical realm; so it is in the spiritual. We all must learn to walk before we can run, and we need the help of another as our spiritual legs grow stronger. Evidence of our growth is always seen in our *walk*, so be patient.

I adore the ancient meaning for the word interpreted "baptism." Originally, it was used as a description meaning "to stain," as one would dye a piece of cloth. I love this. I envision an artist taking a clean white piece of cloth and purposefully gently laying it down into a bright red dye. As it is immersed, the article fully absorbs the crimson fluid, saturating every fiber with an intentional purpose. It now has been completely altered into an entirely different cloth color. No longer can this piece of fabric be considered the same for it has now been changed in identity into the color of the dye that has covered it. No ounce of this weave was exempt when washed.

Surrendering our lives for Him, we kneel at the altar and arise altered. When we step into the waters of baptism, we identify ourselves anew as one who has been spiritually cleansed and washed in the crimson blood of Jesus Christ, inside and out, through every fiber of our being. We are permanently blood-stained. We have not only been dyed but rather our old life *has* died forever so that we can now walk resurrected.

"Baptized" also means "to make whelmed," and though the word "whelmed" is not one often used, I appreciate the context here. That is exactly how we feel when we surrender to God's loving grace and mercy. We are wonderfully and most gloriously *overwhelmed* when we plunge into His loving arms. God's love whelms us as he covers us with a new robe of righteousness. Because of the blood of Christ, it is no longer our old filthy rags but His love covering us that God sees.

When a pure change of heart in the disciple of Jesus Christ is lived out in the resurrected walk, the world takes notice. Those saturated wet feet of baptism will be tracking water marks all the way to the Father's home.

JOURNAL your thoughts on how your life has shown the love of God penetrating the deepest fibers of your being.

_____

_____

_____

_____

_____

_____

_____

_____

_____

_____

_____

_____

_____

_____

_____

_____

_____

_____

DAY 9

The World Takes Notice

"Now as they observed the confidence of Peter and John and understood that they were uneducated and untrained men, they were amazed, and began to recognize them as having been with Jesus."

Acts 4:13 (NASB)

In the book of Acts, as the apostles Peter and John were teaching the people and proclaiming that in Jesus was the resurrection of the dead, the authorities continued to take notice. They could not help but pay attention. Signs were following the Word preached, and healings and miracles resulted.

Soon their audience enlarged to about 5,000 believers. How could anyone overlook such a wild fire? It was the obvious flame the prophet Jeremiah proclaimed: "But if I say, I will not remember Him or speak anymore in His name. Then in my heart it becomes like a burning fire shut up in my bones" (Jeremiah 10:9, NASB). This spiritual wildfire could not be contained within the apostles, and it should not be contained in us now.

Eventually, what the authorities thought was a "disturbance" caused quite a stir and unfortunately this resulted in the arrest of Peter and John. Though fishers of men, this type of catch and release landing them in prison was probably getting old. I bet that this was not their preferred means of having a captive audience to witness their testimony, but God had other plans. They trusted Him and the world took notice.

"Now as they observed the confidence of Peter and John and understood that they were uneducated and untrained men, they were amazed, and began to recognize them as having been with Jesus" (Acts 4:13, NASB).

In this verse, the council could not help but notice that they had *been with Jesus*. This statement inspires my heart with courage every time I read it. Their confidence was not hidden; it was publicly seen. But note, they were not bold because of any educational degree or world training in head knowledge, but rather it was their heart knowledge that was observed by all. Remember that both of these men actually had been with Jesus in the flesh. These disciples of Christ knew Jesus because they had spent time with Him and had fostered a deep relationship with Him.

The word "Christian" often simply defined as a *follower of Christ*, actually comes from the combination of two Greek words. One implies *the walk* as we have previously discussed, and the other exposes who the walk is *with*.

"Christos" is the obvious identification with Jesus Christ, but this word has a deeper implication. It also gives evidence of who one walks alongside with. "Christos" is also defined as the "Messiah, Christ, the Anointed One."

Stay there for a moment with me: "Christos" = "the anointed one." The beauty of this definition is found in the Greek word "Chrio" that "Christos" comes from, meaning "to smear or rub with oil." And get this: through the idea of <u>contact</u>. If there is no contact, there is no anointing oil. This anointing oil is sacred and used to consecrate a sacrifice. So as the disciples walked closely with Jesus, it was as if they walked shoulder to shoulder with Him. The Anointed One ("Christos") had "rubbed off" ("Chrio") on them and His holy presence was evident to all. What a sweet fragrance!

It was certainly obvious to the council that Peter and John had been with Jesus because they were filled with the Holy Spirit, speaking freely and courageously about someone they closely knew. By spending so much time in His company, the passion of Christ remained kindled and it burned strong. They could not bear to keep it inside and neither should we.

We, too, need to fuel our passion for our Lord by rubbing shoulders with Jesus daily, and soon our confidence will grow stronger with practice. Remember, it is about *who* we know, not *what* we know that makes the difference. Heart knowing is more important than head knowing. However, as disciplined time in His Word increases, the mind begins understanding more and more of what the heart already knows by faith.

As we spend time alone with our Lord, the world will not be able to help but take notice. Burning in our hearts, we will desire to spread this sacred passion to tell the world about our Savior. Because of the evidence of His holy presence in our lives, we too begin looking more and more like Him.

JOURNAL a prayer for someone you know who has been with Jesus this week. Be thankful for how God uses their spiritual embrace to allow the fragrance of Christ to rub off on you.

_____

_____

_____

_____

_____

_____

_____

_____

_____

_____

_____

_____

_____

_____

_____

_____

_____

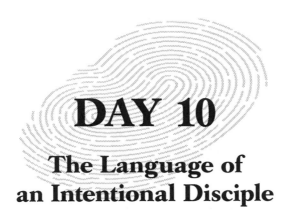

DAY 10

The Language of
an Intentional Disciple

"We love, because He first loved us."

I John 4:19 (NASB)

Throughout the ages, all of mankind has realized that communication is necessary in order to exchange information. For this to take place, a common language must be spoken or written. In God's case, it is both.

1 John 4:16 (NASB) says, "God is love." This precious reminder emphasizes to us that not only does God speak love but He *is* love. The words flowing from our Divine Author are none other than the God-kind of love.

Our Creator so graciously wants us to know Him that He put love into an earth-suit and gave Him the earth name "Jesus." God's living love was therefore demonstrated in the life of Jesus. Love talked. Love walked. Love lived. Right before our eyes, Jesus was God in the flesh.

Just as this life of Jesus visually demonstrates God's love in action as an example for us to follow, so the Bible is God's love language written down to give us "wisdom that leads to salvation through faith which is in Christ Jesus" 2 Timothy 3:15 (NASB).

Learning to speak this love language takes discipline. As an *intentional* disciple of Jesus, Jesus Christ our Lord is the ultimate example that we should compare our manner of life to, not another. Not another believer, not another leader, not another author, pastor, or teacher, but only the example of Jesus Christ as revealed in His holy written Word.

As intentional disciples, we not only learn to speak His language with our mouths but we also learn to live His language with our lives. We love not only in word but also in action of deeds and in truth, according to 1 John 3:18. God demonstrated His love by loving us first, (1 John 4:19) even when we were dead in sins, writes Paul in Ephesians 2:4-6.

Even "while we were still sinners, Christ died for us," Paul repeats in Romans 5:8 (NIV). So if God loved us before we loved Him back, why then do we expect others to look and act perfect before we show God's love to them? You really do have to catch a fish before you clean it. So why do we expect people to be all cleaned up before we communicate the gospel to them? We shouldn't.

I, too, am still growing in this area. Since all of creation reflects the Creator and since all people are created in the image of God, I need to intentionally look for the face of Jesus in every face I see. As we appreciate Him in them, we are more aware of someone whom God loves. We will recognize them as someone for whom Jesus lived and died for.

I will never forget the Sunday morning that I was reading John 3:16 and saw the goodness of God given to all creation in this beloved Scripture: "For God so loved the world, that He gave His Only begotten Son, that whosoever believeth in Him should not Perish, but have Everlasting Life" (KJV).

Reading this verse for the millionth time, this moment was totally different. Six specific letters began to shine boldly as if they were highlighted so bright that there was absolutely no way that I could miss them: **G-O-S-P-E-L**. It was as if the Holy Spirit of God seemed to shine a flashlight on those six individual letters and then I saw it! Yes, this good news of God's love had been there all along but I never saw the *gospel* of Jesus Christ is in this one verse!

"For God so loved the world, that He gave His Only begotten Son, that whosoever believeth in Him should not Perish, but have Everlasting Life" (John 3:16, KJV, emphasis added).

May we more purposefully look for God's face upon the earth in those beautiful faces of earth that our potter has handmade. We must love God more by loving the ones He has made, according to 1 John 4:7-11 (NASB):

> Beloved, let us love one another, for love is from God; and everyone who loves is born of God and knows God. The one who does not love does not know God, for God is love. By this the love of God was manifested in us, that God has sent His only begotten son into the world so that we might live through Him. In this is love, not that we loved God, but that He loved us and sent His Son to be the propitiation for our sins. Beloved, if God so loved us, we also ought to love one another.

If we live God's love out loud to the world, then the world will hear God's love spoken to them through us.

JOURNAL how God's amazing love toward you can teach you how to love others.

_____

_____

_____

_____

_____

_____

_____

_____

_____

_____

_____

_____

_____

_____

_____

_____

_____

_____

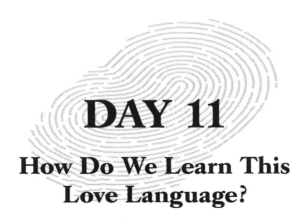

DAY 11

How Do We Learn This Love Language?

"A new commandment I give to you, that you love one another, even as I have loved you, that you also love one another. By this all men will know that you are My disciples if you have love for one another."

John 13:34-35 (NASB)

Years ago, churches would often close their worship services with the chorus, "They will know we are Christians by our love." It was a call to arms, not in the military sense, but rather a call to the arms of unity in the surrendered embrace. Biblical love embraces unity. This love is also the distinguishing mark of disciples of Jesus. His followers must authentically love strong or the world may never hear God's call for them.

Yesterday, we discovered that love, simply put, looks like Jesus. Speaking to His disciples, Jesus explained, "This is My commandment, that you love one another, just I have loved you" (John 15:12, NASB). But where do we go to see how Jesus loved, and how do we learn this love language? By spending time with the author and teacher of course. Spending time with the words of God in the Word of God, the Bible, we are taught ways to put these verbal expressions into action.

Since every language in the world is made up of words containing meaning, why would we expect this heavenly language to be anything different? The Bible is where we must diligently go to find this love language filled with our words of meaning. It is our Heavenly Father who has written His love letters to His beloved children.

Our desire to intimately know Jesus motivates us to personally invest in learning time. This is referred to by many as a "quiet time" or a "devotional." If you need a starting place for Bible study, I encourage you to begin reading from the beloved apostle John's writings in the New Testament. The Gospel of John and 1st, 2nd and 3rd John are beautiful passages of Scripture to nourish your heart, resulting in spiritual growth. Not only will these words convince you of how much you are loved, but they will also teach you how to love others.

As we start prioritizing more and more time spent within the Scriptures, we are more likely to start living by the Word. Time *in* the Word results in time *with* the Word. The more that the Word is *in* us, the more of the Word is *with* us. Thus, making God's Word our dwelling place or habitation, He takes up residence in every area of our life. As we continue to abide with Him, He abides with us. "If you keep My commandments, you will abide in My love; just as I have kept My Father's commandments and abide in His love" (John 15:10).

In order to keep God's commandments, we must first learn what they are. Though it is not always easy to study scripture, we must remember that we are never alone as we do. Just as God speaks to us through His written Word, He also has given us His Holy Spirit to be our interpreter and guide in the truth. We must however give Him time to teach us.

One needs to discipline themselves daily in transitioning from a mere duty to a pure delight of God's Word. Pastor Bob Roberts of Northwood Church in Keller, Texas reinforces this purposeful practice during one of his Sunday sermons. *"Discipleship is not easy... Discipline is the root of Discipleship. Discipline moves us from contemplating the right choices to doing the right things... Only discipline allows someone to know God deeply."*

Going deeper may get uncomfortable in the beginning. And yes, digging into the Word may get messy on some days. We may awkwardly realize that our hands are quite dirty as His light exposes our sin. Friend, in the end, we will understand that it was worth it. Self-discipline will be rewarded with beauty beyond compare. Eventually, God's Word will change us from what we were into becoming what He created us to be. By intentionally spending time with Him, we genuinely display His love to others.

JOURNAL your desire to spend time with the Author of Love by daily reading His love letters to you. Designate a daily time of reading God's Word and select a starting passage in the Bible.

_____

_____

_____

_____

_____

_____

_____

_____

_____

_____

_____

_____

_____

_____

_____

_____

_____

_____

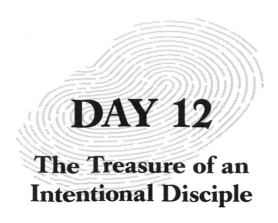

DAY 12

The Treasure of an Intentional Disciple

"Where your treasure is, there your heart will be also."

Matthew 6:21 (NASB)

As we have seen, it is in the daily reading of God's Word, where intentional disciples learn to speak the Heavenly King's language of love. Appreciating the value of these cherished moments will also allow jewels to be discovered from the kingdom of heaven (Matthew 13:44).

It is said that when looking at someone's checkbook or bank account, a person's value system can be identified. Maybe we should personalize that. Where do we spend the majority of our time? What are our priority purchases? In the Gospel of Matthew, Jesus instructed His disciples not to store up earthly items of wealth but rather to choose to gather our treasures in heaven where only God sees them. The values we place on earthly things do seem to identify what we most value if we are not careful.

Previously in Day four, we examined how Jesus dwells within the spiritual home of our heart once He has been invited to live there. As we cherish His letters from heaven and read them and reread them, He makes a difference, room by room. As we live with the Word, the Word becomes lived out in us.

Applying God's Word to this, Psalm 119:11 deepens our understanding of this principle: "Your Word I have treasured in my heart..." Just as we make a financial deposit into our earthly bank accounts in order to make a sufficient withdrawal, so we also must invest time storing the treasure of God's Word into our hearts. Our Father graciously encourages us to draw upon God's promises in His Holy Word. But what about when your Bible is not with you or the internet is down so there is nowhere to retrieve from? Then it will be time to draw upon saved resources that are hopefully within our hearts.

Valuing God's Word enough to store it as a treasure within will never disappoint. *Dwell on the Word of God and it will dwell within you.* One of those glorious treasures is freedom. In John 8:31-32 (NASB), Jesus was speaking with believers as He said, "If you continue in My word, then you are truly disciples of mine; and you will know the truth, and the truth will make you free."

Please realize that it is not just about owning a copy of the Bible that is spoken of here, but it is in our *knowing* the Word of God. Knowing the truth that is found in the Word of God is where true freedom is found. I emphasize once more. *Dwell on the Word of God and it will dwell within you.*

I am absolutely not intending to communicate that our salvation is completely dependent on the minutes of our quiet time. It is, however, an evidence of how much our relationship with our Heavenly Father is worth to us and if we desire for it to grow stronger. I confess that practicing self-examination, I ask myself how my spiritual "trust fund" is looking. Am I trusting God or myself more this week? The evidence will always be revealed in my time treasury.

The second part of Psalm 119:11 reveals why David adores God's Word so much. First and foremost, David deeply loves God and wants to be near Him. David longs to listen to Him and therefore loves the words that God has spoken. But David also realizes that those words can actually save his life and prevent him from sinning. The New International Version translates it with clarity: "I have hidden your word in my heart that I might not sin against you."

Because a pure and holy heart is priceless before our Holy God, sin cannot stand in God's presence… only holiness. It is by clinging to the treasure of God's Word in the depths of our heart that we, like David, can learn how to remove obstacles that could hinder our intimacy with God.

God's desire is that we desire more of Him. I think that is one reason that in 1 Samuel 13:14 and Acts 13:22, King David was called "a man after my own heart" by God Himself. Even though David's life was filled with challenges, he earnestly desired to please His God even when his actions did not seem like it. This may be one reason so many of us identify with David in the Bible. One such prayer is found in 2 Samuel 7:18-29. The posture of David's heart can be seen throughout his life. Even when he fell down, he would reach out to the Lord. God graciously always seemed to know his heart's motive, and God graciously sees each of ours.

The word that is translated "hidden" also means "preserved or saved." The comparison is that this valuable treasure, when kept close to one's heart, will be more difficult for thieves to steal. By holding it close, not only are we protecting it from theft but also we are saving it for ourselves. Jesus is not just our Savior in the past, but His Word saves us every day.

Leaning into the "preserved" meaning of "hidden", visualize someone canning fruits or vegetables. The whole reason that we preserve fruit that is in season is so that we can open it up and use it in times of need when it is not so readily available. Disciples also can intentionally be instant in season and out of season. 2 Timothy 4:2 reminds us to stay prepared to "preach the word; be ready in season and out of season" (NASB). We can retrieve the Word at just the right time as the Holy Spirit brings it back to our mind. Being instant with speaking a word in season may very well be the method that the Holy Spirit will use in you to overflow and share His love. I encourage you to remain ready and filled. Take advantage of the fruitful seasons of life and there will be more jars in the cupboard for seasons of need.

"The Counselor, the Holy Spirit, whom the Father will send in my name, will teach you all things and will remind you of everything I have said to you" (John 14:26, NASB). In this passage, our Father God, in Jesus' name, has given the Holy Spirit to us as a helper. It is He who reminds us of God's Word when we forget them; however, He can only bring to our remembrance those things that we have taken time to learn. May we intentionally hide, preserve, and save those jewels in our hearts, knowing that they will brilliantly surface at just the right time.

JOURNAL what Psalm 119:11 personally means to you. "Your word I have treasured in my heart, that I may not sin against You." Commit an action to follow that desire to allow His Word to come alive in you.

_____

_____

_____

_____

_____

_____

_____

_____

_____

_____

_____

_____

_____

_____

_____

_____

_____

_____

_____

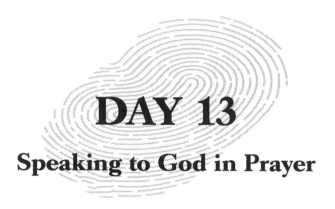

DAY 13
Speaking to God in Prayer

"Call to me and I will answer you and tell you great
and unsearchable things you do not know."

Jeremiah 33:3 (NIV)

All communication involves an exchange of information. It is two-way; otherwise, it is not actual conversation. Listening to God speak to us through His holy written Word is one way that He talks to us daily. By God's grace, we also are invited to talk to Him. This is simply called prayer.

We can speak to God anytime and anywhere, as we would an honored friend. During this devotion time, our Heavenly Father will also speak to us if we will get quiet. To me, that is the hard part. I really like to talk and I know that He loves to listen, but God has a lot to say. If I am not careful, I could miss it.

Never underestimate God's timing or method. He is creative and may answer prayers even through a song, a note from a friend, or a sermon, etc. His voice may be as a whisper within your heart, or He may even answer at an unusual time that seems strange, like when you are vacuuming or taking a shower. Then all of a sudden, you know the answer to a previous question deep within you.

We think we are waiting on Him but often it is He who is waiting on us. Leaving space for grace is important. Sometimes, He has just been waiting for our mind to get quiet, and when we least expect it, we will hear His voice. Maybe this is why times of devotion are often called "quiet time."

Every breath we take reveals that we are dependent on God and that we cannot do life on our own. God knows that we need Him but sometimes we don't. Our needs are actually a gift. God allows us to have needs so that we recognize our ultimate need is *Him*. This special time with God in prayer provides opportunity for us to share the secrets of our heart, bring needs for ourselves or others to Him, and deeply engage in intimate conversation.

God actually knows us better than we know ourselves. He wants us to call out to Him. This unveiling is precious. In prayer, He can speak to us concerning our known and unknown needs. We must trust His yes and His no because only God knows what needs we will have for the future that only He sees. As it's written in Jeremiah 33:3, "Call to me and I will answer you, and will tell you great and hidden things that you have not known" (ESV).

There have been many times that I have wondered why life did not go the way I had hoped. Afterward, I realized that I never did stop to ask God for His directions. No wonder I got off track. This is another reason we come to God in prayer. Prayer is simply calling on God by speaking to Him, in reverence, as we seek direction for our lives. It is like a soldier in battle who calls into headquarters to get orders and guidance for strategy to know what to do. God always has a plan, but we must request His instructions. We need to just stop and humbly ask.

In Matthew 7:7, Jesus reminds us to ask Him for His help: "**A**sk, and it will be given to you; **S**eek, and you will find; **K**nock, and the door will be opened to you" (NIV, emphasis added). Not only is "ask" found in this Scripture, it also is found in the first letter of each action word. We all need the reminder, so ASK is doubly emphasized.

Prayer also gives us an opportunity to thank Him and glorify Him. The following promise of Jesus in John 15:7-8 (NASB) confirms that as we ask according to His will, He answers.

> If you abide in Me, and My words abide in you, ask
> whatever you wish, and it will be done for you. My
> Father is glorified by this, that you bear much fruit,
> and so prove to be My disciples.

"According to His will" is the same as the agreement of the Scriptures. By spending time in the Word of God, we learn what His will looks like in situations. His Word and His will always agree. If ever there is doubt regarding a decision, give priority to the Scriptures. If the answer is printed in the Bible, then know the answer has already been given.

The result is that this answered prayer, according to His will, bears the spiritual fruit of joy. This praise brings glory to God the Father and results in great joy for us. God gets glory and we receive joy!

Let's continue by unpacking some principles to build a stronger foundation for prayer.

Why do we even need to pray?

- Prayer strengthens our spirit to be stronger than our flesh. Prayer helps us to have the mind of Christ to hear God guiding us and keeping us strong to withstand the temptations of the evil one. Matthew 26:41 says, "Watch and pray so that you will not fall into temptation. The spirit is willing, but the body is weak" (NIV).
- In Matthew 6:8, it says that God already knows what we need. So why, then, do we need to pray? Because prayer is not when God finds out about our needs; it is when we finally decide to give them to Him. God receives the glory for answered prayers, which strengthens our faith and increases our joy.

How do we pray?

- In both John 16:23 and Matthew 6:9, among other verses of Scripture, we are told to pray unto God our Father, not someone else. This was modeled by Jesus Himself in what has become known as the Lord's Prayer, found in Matthew 6:9-13.

- In John 14:13-14, we are instructed to pray to the Father in the name of Jesus, for it is by His blood that we are allowed to enter.
- We are to pray with a heart posture of both humility and confidence. Each of us can come near to God in prayer and with reverence. Our access comes in knowing that only Jesus is truly holy enough to enter God's presence. Since He alone is worthy, it is only by His blood and in His name that we dare to draw near. Accepting His payment for our sin, we are able to gloriously enter the throne room of grace with full assurance of faith, boldly drawing near with sincere hearts (Hebrews 10:19, 22). Oh, what mercy! What grace! Our Heavenly Father deems no need too small for a child of His to enter.
- Once we have prayed, we watch with joyful expectation for His answer. Remember to thank Him for hearing you and having His Will done. Trust His timing and use your faith while you are in the waiting room. As it's written in Colossians 4:2, "Devote yourselves to prayer, keeping alert in it with an attitude of thanksgiving" (NASB).

What kind of things can we pray for?

- We can pray for boldness to speak God's Word (Colossians 4:4).
- We pray for forgiveness (1 John 1:9).
- As we continue to grow in our faith, we pray for holiness and faith to accompany our prayers (1 Timothy 2:8, Hebrews 10:14).

The Bible also comforts us that even in those times when we do not know how or what to pray, both Jesus and the Holy Spirit are praying for us. We find this promise in John 17:20, Romans 8:26-27, and Hebrews 7:25.

Continue to remain honest and transparent with Father God as you pray. After all, He has already read your heart and knows just what you want to say even before a word is uttered. Just trust Him. He loves you more than you could ever imagine and longs to give good gifts to His children. Matthew 7:11 says, "Your Father who is in heaven gives what is good to those who ask Him" (NASB).

JOURNAL a prayer to Father God focusing on His throne of grace. See Jesus at the door for you, inviting you to enter. Receive His mercy and ask for His help during your time of need right now.

_____

_____

_____

_____

_____

_____

_____

_____

_____

_____

_____

_____

_____

_____

_____

_____

_____

DAY 14

Evidence of Our Love for God

"This is love for God: to obey his commands. And his commands are not burdensome."

1 John 5:3 (NIV)

As we savor our opportunities to speak with God in prayer, let's never take them for granted. When we enter His presence with an attitude of gratitude and thanksgiving, not only are we to gratefully praise God for all He has done, but we also need to sincerely worship Him for all that He is. Desiring His heart more than His hand reveals who we are most focused on—Him or us?

So how do we show God that we love Him? Just as a disciple proves that he or she is a follower of Jesus Christ by their love, so it is our obedience to what God's Word says that demonstrates our love for Him. My mom always said, "Actions speak louder than words." Can this also relate to our relationship with God? Absolutely yes. What does the genuine love of a disciple look like to God? The answer is found in our obedience. Obedience is our *love in action*, as stated in 2 John 1:6, "this is love: that we walk in obedience to his commands" (NIV).

I cannot help but remember when this truth came alive for me personally. Years ago, I was teaching a class of four-year-olds at a Christian preschool. One little boy, we'll call Christopher was so certain that he would get a "time out" at some point in the day—based on his interactions with other students—that he began planting toys near the designated spot. I distinctly remember one day when he called me over while in the time out spot. As I squatted down to look into his big blue eyes, he said, "Ms. Sherry, I love you." I replied, "I love you, too, but Christopher, if you loved me, then you would do what I say." I tenderly hugged him and walked away to let those words soak in. Immediately, the Holy Spirit ever so gently whispered in my ear, "Sherry, if you love me, you will do what I say too." I so got the message, and now, many, many years later, I still remember. Unfortunately, I do not always obey what God says the first time either and then, just like my little learner, I too get a "time out."

Believe me when I say that I have had plenty of "time outs." Obviously, God also believes in time outs when we disobey Him. Just look at the story of Jonah in the Old Testament if you ever doubt it. Out of His great love and compassion, God kindly leads us to repentance. Like Jonah, we must first stop running and come to the point of repentance by truly being sorry for bad choices of disobedience. By humbly coming to our senses and admitting our mistake, we too can ask God to forgive us. By His grace, He will. Our loving Father so desires for us to have a close relationship with Him that He continues to make a way for all prodigals to run back to our home of grace once we find His road of mercy.

Loving the Lord our God with all our heart, all our soul, and all our strength is demonstrated in our serious obedience to choosing God's Word and God's Will over our own will. In John 14:23-24, we read, "Anyone who loves me will obey my teaching. My Father will love them, and we will come to them and make our home with them. Anyone who does not love me will not obey my teaching" (NIV).

Those strong words reveal that obedience obviously matters to God. One example can be found in 1 Samuel 15:22. There was a time when King Saul chose not to accept the specifics of God's directions in a matter. He decided to do something good for God when God wanted his best.

Because of this rebellious act of disobedience, Saul is addressed by the prophet Samuel. Speaking on behalf of God, Samuel states, "to obey is better than sacrifice." This reminds us that it is not what we think God would like that shows our love for Him, but rather it is in our submissive actions to His Word that gives the evidence of our heart. Obedience is love displayed in our actions.

Walking out God's directions for our lives is always safer when we follow His lead. Notice that I did not say easier but *safer*! Should He lead you into the valley of the shadow of death, you will fear no evil, for, as Psalm 23 comforts, He is with you. By intentionally focusing on His presence abiding with us, fear surrenders to faith.

Knowing and following God's presence is following His will. As long as the Lord is the one leading, you are in the safest place possible. However, if He guides a turn to the right and we disobey and go left, there could be a season of consequences following that choice where we cannot see the Lord clearly. Remember, dear friend, that He has not left us. Deuteronomy 31:6 assures us that God will never leave us or forsake us; however, there may be times that we have temporarily left Him.

As an intentional disciple of Jesus, it is easier to do what He says when we can actually hear what He is saying, so I encourage you to walk closely. His voice will always be heard loudest when we are nearest to Him. But if you find yourself in a place where you feel you took a wrong turn, just go back to the last place that He was with you. Just like a lost child in a store, He listens for you to cry out for Him and soon He will be there to embrace you with His loving arms. Glean from the experience. Learn to hold His hand tighter, stay closer, and keep walking.

JOURNAL an example of how your love for Father God is being displayed at the present and if a "time out" needs to be called. If so, allow this to be yours.

_____

_____

_____

_____

_____

_____

_____

_____

_____

_____

_____

_____

_____

_____

_____

_____

_____

DAY 15

What on Earth Does Love Like?

"The fruit of the Spirit is love, joy, peace, forbearance, kindness, goodness, faithfulness, gentleness and self-control ..."

Galatians 5:22-23 (NIV)

In this journey of discipleship, we have discovered again and again that love is the main characteristic of a disciple of Jesus. The golden rule in Matthew 7:12 says, "So in everything, do to others what you would have them do to you…" As we treat others as we would want to be treated, the world not only experiences our love for them, but they also experience God's love for them as well. His attributes are being displayed in and through us since He lives within our hearts.

Nature itself displays the love of God. Though people may feel His majestic presence in creation, they may not know the One who spoke it into being. Creation reveals the Creator, and His hand is seen in everything that He has made, including His people made in His image. "For since the creation of the world His invisible attributes, His eternal power and divine nature, have been clearly seen, being understood through what has been made, so that they are without excuse," says Romans 1:20 (NASB).

In Matthew 12:33, Jesus teaches one such truth: "The tree is known by its fruit." Both physically and spiritually, this undeniable fact proves that the outward evidence of a tree cannot be questioned. The fruit produced just proves what already exists within the seed.

Since the manifestation of the love of Jesus includes consistent fruitfulness displayed through us, conducting periodic self-examinations from time to time may be needed. As Psalm 26:2 probes, "Examine me, O Lord, and try me; Test my mind and my heart" (NASB). Putting this into practice, I ask myself, "Is my life tree producing fruit during this season? Exactly what kind of fruit is actually hanging around on my branches for others? Is it barely ripe, is it fully ripened, or Lord forbid, is it rotten?" You see, self-inspection allows the light of the Holy Spirit to highlight any areas needing special attention. "But you know me, O Lord; You see me; And you examine my heart's attitude toward You" (Jeremiah 12:3, NASB). Once any needs are identified, focusing on their improvement will be more likely.

We must be careful not to compare ourselves to others in this area because no two spiritual gardens will grow at the same rate. Though every believer has been given fruit by the Holy Spirit, each one unwraps their gift differently. Our responsibility is not to prune someone else's tree but rather to water, feed, and nourish the fruit on ours. Our focus should be on becoming more like Christ Jesus and not someone else.

In Galatians 5:22-23, the fruit of the Holy Spirit are specifically listed. The word *fruit*, whether singular or plural, emphasizes that God is Love and the fruit of His Holy Spirit is love. This love is demonstrated with the evidence of a fruitful spiritual life. God's love demonstrated through our lives is manifested as joy, peace, long-suffering, gentleness, goodness, faith, meekness, and temperance, or self-control.

The following commentary on Galatians 5:22-23 given in the King James Version of the Open Bible beautifully identifies the fruit of the Spirit as *love*. Creatively revealing what God's love looks like in the world through an intentional disciple is unveiled line by line.

"The fruit of the Spirit is LOVE.
Joy is love's strength.
Peace is love's security.

Long-suffering is love's patience or endurance.
Gentleness is love's conduct.
Goodness is love's character.
Faith is love's confidence.
Meekness is love's humility.
Temperance is love's victory."

The more that I ponder the beauty of this description, the more it witnesses with my heart. Our spiritual fruit displayed on earth continues to be the outward evidence of what is growing within our hearts. I pray that our deeper roots will produce sweeter fruit. May we make it our aim for the world to see and hear Christ through the fruitfulness of His Love in us.

JOURNAL your decision to live love out loud by displaying the fruit of the Spirit. Give yourself a personal fruit inspection by thinking of examples of each. Carefully identify any areas needing special attention and ask God to help you make any changes necessary.

_____

_____

_____

_____

_____

_____

_____

_____

_____

_____

_____

_____

_____

_____

_____

_____

_____

DAY 16

About Face

"I hope to visit you and talk with you face to face, so that our joy may be complete."

2 John 1:12 (NIV)

We have all heard the old saying that "You only get one chance to make a good first impression". An initial introduction may or may not be an accurate summation of a person's character or true personality, but it usually does expose a person's mood. Proverbs 15:13 reminds us that "A joyful heart makes a cheerful face" (NASB). Since one of the fruit of the Spirit is joy, Christ followers should be the happiest people on earth, in my opinion, because they actually have something to smile about.

When our heart is overflowing with endless reasons to be thankful, our external expressions can't help but respond to the condition of our overflowing hearts. As we remind ourselves of the joy of our salvation (Psalm 51:12), we are also to rejoice in the God of our salvation! Believers are to "rejoice that our names are written in heaven" (Luke 10:20, NIV) and to be glad, for "The Lord has done great things for us, and we are filled with joy" (Psalm 126:3, NIV).

An added bonus is that this kind of joy is not only contagious but also healthy, as Proverbs 17:22 confirms: "A merry heart does good, *like* medicine, But a broken spirit dries the bones" (NKJV). Physically, when we smile, the brain releases the feel-good neurotransmitters known as dopamine, endorphins, and serotonin into the body. These are the important brain chemicals that boost our happy feelings. And not only do they affect our mood and concentration, but these chemicals also benefit us by relieving pain and stress. Not only will smiling result in our looking happier on the outside, but it will also result in our spiritual temple being healthier on the inside. No wonder it feels so good when you're smiling!

Not only are we to experience joy but also to "re-joy," or rejoice, no matter what. To rejoice means to experience joy again and again, as in Philippians 4:4. We are actually told to be joyful, rejoice, have joy, take joy, etc. at least 100 times in the Bible. God must have known we needed reminders. If "the joy of the Lord is your strength" (Nehemiah 8:10, KJV), then the contrast reveals that our lack of joy could actually become the cause of our weakness as well. If we had been told to be joyful only one time by our Father God, it would have been enough; however, He emphasizes it over 100 times! Well, that shows me that He knows us well.

The face of a disciple should reflect the heart of the disciple. Genuine joy results from having God-given peace in one's heart, knowing that His presence is with us no matter what we go through. Though happiness may be a result of circumstances, joy is constant. Spiritual joy is not an emotional feeling that fluctuates with unstable wavering or moodiness; rather, it is a state of heart that does not change according to situations. It actually remains ever constant in spite of them. Our joy is not demonstrated because of our circumstances but rather in spite of them.

"O satisfy us in the morning with Your lovingkindness, that we may sing for joy and be glad all our days," says Psalm 90:14 (NASB). This verse does not imply that we are to sing for joy only on the days when it seems that everything is going perfect (after all, when is that really?) but quite the contrary. "Sing for joy and be glad *all* our days!" We are told to rejoice and be glad at all times, even in times of persecution or tribulation (Matthew 5:12, 2 Corinthians 7:4).

But how do we remain glad all of our days? By intentionally centering our thoughts on the joy of our salvation. Not basing feelings on circumstances, King David in the Psalms realized that worshipping God invited the presence of God into his circumstances. No matter the ups and downs of life, he was convinced that God never changes, even when circumstances do.

David also knew that being near the heart of God would bring him clarity. After a season of brokenness, David cried out and asked God to restore him. He sought God to give him strength even in times when feelings were absent, but he wanted to have a willing spirit for them to return: "Restore to me the joy of Your salvation and sustain me with a willing spirit" (Psalm 51:12, NASB).

Our focus is what determines the measure of our joy, not our feelings. When Jesus is the object of our affection, He is the object of our ultimate joy. Our joy will *not* be circumstantial when our focus is on Jesus because God is our stronghold and refuge. We have this reason to sing. "Let us rejoice and be glad in his salvation" (Isaiah 25:9).

JOURNAL what reasons you have to be joyful and allow the image of Christ to be mirrored as a reflection in you to the world today.

_____

_____

_____

_____

_____

_____

_____

_____

_____

_____

_____

_____

_____

_____

_____

_____

_____

_____

DAY 17

Family Reunions

"And let us consider how we may spur one another on toward love and good deed, not giving up meeting together, as some are in the habit of doing, but encouraging one another— and all the more as you see the Day approaching."

Hebrews 10:24-25 (NIV)

Born in Mississippi, I have had my share of family reunions where hospitality abounds. But it can feel uncomfortable when you first step in the door. Somehow, this unique experience initially seems like an awkward mosaic of strangers who know that they are related but somehow must learn how to relate with courtesy. Please don't take this wrong, but to me, personally, this image is similar to our spiritual family called the church. Diverse groups of people filled with dysfunction come together weekly while enjoying delicious food, wonderful music, and fellowship together. The difference is the reason that we come and who we are celebrating.

Growing in the grace and knowledge of our Lord Jesus Christ is always easier when supported by a mature spiritual family. The church location does not matter. The Bible does. According to John 4:21, worship is not a "where" but a "who" and "how." The building or place is not the reason for a spiritual family to gather. Rather than attending a building to worship God, we bring our worship with us. It is not the responsibility of a praise team to help us "get our praise on." A good service is not dependent on the song selection. No. We don't come to a church service to start worshipping; rather, we should come to the church *already worshipping.* We come together in our spiritual community to intentionally focus on our God who is worthy of praise. He is the guest of honor and we are to be honored by His presence.

Our family of faith gathering together is a beautiful picture of love working within relationships. A group of people earnestly longing for the companionship of a friend to do life with will likely build bonds of fellowship with many other believers in the process. Be careful, though; growing our social life should never take priority over growing our spiritual life, so keep those motives in check.

This healthy picture of the living body of Christ is complete when the believers join together in unity with Jesus Christ as the head. The family of believers gather to worship God and infuse strength in each other as they learn the Holy Scriptures and their applications. When prayer needs arrive, mature believers help younger ones surrender their concerns at the foot of the cross. Opportunities to serve are always encouraged within a growing church, and ministries abound to exercise the strengths that each individual member has been equipped with. You never regret bringing your best gift to offer as a living sacrifice to the Lord.

What about those challenging times when you just don't feel like going to church? In Hebrews 10:25, we are exhorted to "not give up meeting together, as some are in the habit of doing, but let us encourage one another and all the more as you see the Day approaching." There have been days when I honestly felt that prying my tired body out of bed was my living sacrifice, spoken of in Romans 12:1. But listen to the words of Hebrews 13:15: "Through Jesus, therefore, let us continually offer to God a sacrifice of praise—the fruit of lips that openly confess his name" (NIV). This tells me that our heartfelt praise is our sacrifice. The Holy Spirit can even do His work during quiet moments of praise. Some of the sweetest worship that I have ever experienced arrived in times of silent meditation upon Him, unspeakable joy full of glory (1 Peter 1:8).

In Psalm 21:6 and Psalm 16:11, we are told that it is in God's presence that we find our fullness of joy. The Lord rewards our faithfulness, so if there are moments that we need more joy in our lives, we should get into His presence all the more, not less. This is one of many reasons that creating an atmosphere of praise and worship in song is so mighty. 1 Corinthians 3:6 reminds us that our body is the temple of the Holy Spirit living within, so don't reserve worship only for the church sanctuary building. Our worship invites God to sit and to dwell among us, for He inhabits the praises of His people. Our praises create a throne for God Himself to sit upon and abide in a holy habitation, states Psalm 22:3. We, the body of Christ, are His temple, created as His dwelling place (1 Corinthians 6:19, 20).

Next time you go to your spiritual family reunion, wash your hands, bring your best to share, and know that there will always be a seat at the table waiting for you.

JOURNAL how the being in the family of God can be an encouragement to you and meditate on a practical example of how you can be that for another.

_____

_____

_____

_____

_____

_____

_____

_____

_____

_____

_____

_____

_____

_____

_____

_____

_____

_____

DAY 18
Spiritual Gifts

"Since we have gifts that differ according to the grace given
to us, each of us is to exercise them accordingly..."

Romans 12:6 (NASB)

Our Heavenly Father has been generously bestowing love on us from the beginning with His Son. In John 14:17, Jesus tells the disciples that the Holy Spirit, who has been "with you," will be "in you." These words first came to life once Jesus died, resurrected, and ascended up into heaven, then sent the Holy Spirit down to earth. The Holy Spirit of God initially came to indwell the disciples of Jesus on the day of Pentecost, as recorded in Acts 2:1-17. He continues to live within the human spirit of believers today at their moment of salvation.

Not only does every born-again child of God have God's living Spirit at home within them, but they are also blessed with one or more gifts of the Holy Spirit referred to in the Scriptures as spiritual gifts. Passages such as Romans 12:6-8, Ephesians 4:11-13, and 1 Corinthians 12-15 list many such gifts: prophecy, service, teaching, exhorting, giving, leading, showing mercy, pastoring, evangelizing.

Each of us must learn to gently unwrap these gifts that have been given to share with the family of God on earth. Ephesians 4:12 identifies God's intent for these gifts to be used: "for the equipping of the saints for the work of service to the building up of the body of Christ" (NASB). Each one has received a special gift *as He wills*.

> As each one has received a special gift, employ it in serving one another as good stewards of the manifold grace of God.
>
> –1 Peter 4:10, NASB

God knows best how we can serve Him best. Each spiritual gift fulfills a specific function by the will of the Father. They are for a purpose—*His purpose*. 1 Corinthians 12:18 clarifies that "God has placed the members, each one of them, in the body just as *He* desired" (NASB, emphasis added). Placed as He desired, not necessarily as we desired. This passage reminds us that our role is not to grumble about what talent-present God did or did not gift us with; rather, we are to strongly use what glorifies Him to the very best of our ability.

1 Corinthians 12:11 also states that the manifestation of the Spirit is distributed to each one individually just as God wills for the common good of all. He gives gifts to us according to how He made us. Be encouraged. He knows that we have it in us to do these things for His glory because it is He who put it there inside of us. Trust the Giver; He made you.

We are all individual members of Christ's body and each have a uniquely gifted ability, endowed by God the Father, to encourage and edify His body, the church. In Romans 12:6-8, we are reminded that just as the physical body has differing parts, so does the spiritual body of Christ. Our human body has various parts such as hands, eyes, feet, and each carry with it a different job description. As the spiritual body of Christ walks in His love, the entire body grows stronger. When each member does its part whole-heartedly for the Lord, the entire body grows more in love with Christ the Head.

Learning to faithfully grow and intentionally exercise these grace gifts of the Spirit does take time. This process of maturing in our faith is easier when shared with fellow believers in the faith. Just because someone has a tool or equipment does not always mean that they know how to use it. Gathering with stronger believers provides opportunities to exercise these gifts. Our church community can be like a spiritual body-building gym where the entire body of Christ grows up to be more like Jesus Christ.

Exercising your spiritual gifts is the way that God has endowed and equipped you to fulfill your part of the Great Commission. Rather than fearfully letting them just sit there, let's courageously be a body full of moving parts! When we are unified as one, walking worthy of our callings, we can practice loving and serving God's people. As we earnestly desire spiritual gifts, we are all the more urged to intentionally pursue love. Without love, all other gifts would be pointless. The greatest gift to anyone, anytime, anywhere is always love.

JOURNAL: What spiritual gift do you feel is a strength for you? Ask the Holy Spirit to reveal this if you are not sure.

_____

_____

_____

_____

_____

_____

_____

_____

_____

_____

_____

_____

_____

_____

_____

_____

_____

_____

_____

DAY 19

Called to Freedom

"If you continue in my word, then are you my disciples indeed; and you shall know the truth, and the truth shall make you free."

John 8:31-32 (KJV)

An intentional disciple of Jesus Christ must push beyond inevitable times of difficulty. This journey of commitment is not for the faint of heart. Don't get me wrong, I know that there will be seasons of weakness, but struggles can help identify where we need more strength. Dear warrior, brave the fight. Lift that weight. Cast it off and stand firm in your faith! Christ gives you the strength as a child of God. Agree with Philippians 4:13 and say, "I can do everything through him who gives me strength." By taking His promise to heart, you will faithfully put it into action.

In the introductory Scripture, John 8:31, Jesus declares valuable wisdom. "If you *continue* in my word, then are you my disciples indeed; and you shall know the truth, and the truth shall make you free" (KJV, emphasis added). To continue in the Word is a stark contrast to those who choose not to carry on and pursue the Scriptures. Those with hearts of integrity continue this persistent pursuit of godliness in the Scriptures even when no one else is looking. The energy of steady discipline in God's Word can fuel growth even when feelings are challenged. A pure passion to follow hard after God will ignite the needed endurance to press on and not give up.

This life-changing pattern will soon become a glorious habit with sweet reward. One such benefit is *freedom* and release from bondage!

> It was for freedom that Christ set us free; therefore, keep standing firm and do not be subject again to a life of slavery... For you were called to freedom, brethren; only do not turn your freedom into an opportunity for the flesh, but through love serve one another.
>
> —Galatians 5:1,13, NASB

Hallelujah! The prisoner's cuff has been released! Permission has been granted to no longer be held captive. See those chains laying powerless on the ground. Accept His freedom. Philippians 3:12-15 says, "Forgetting what lies behind and straining forward to what lies ahead, I press on toward the goal for the prize of the upward call of God in Christ Jesus. Let those of us who are mature think this way." The road of freedom is ready to be run for those who let go of those things holding them back.

Review what Jesus said in John 8:31: "If you continue in My word, then you are truly disciples of Mine; and you will *know* the truth, and the truth will make you free" (NASB, emphasis added). Owning a copy of the Word of God is not the same thing as knowing the Word of God. It is only in knowing the truth in God's Word that we are set free.

Learning to apply the Bible's promises to our life will exercise a strong grip of full conviction. 2 Timothy 2:15 states for followers of Christ to "do your best to present yourself to God. Be diligent to present yourself approved to God as a workman who does not need to be ashamed, accurately handling the word of truth" (NASB).

By learning how to cling to what Jesus has said, we can extend faith to believe it. Sacred moments spent holding God's Word tightly in our hearts will leave room for the Word of God to move you. The desire to sin will grow weaker as the depth of our love grows stronger. As my husband puts it, Scripture must go "from head to heart to hand" for true life change to occur. As we read and reread the Holy Word, it eventually becomes the meditation we dwell on within our heart. Once it is in our hearts, God moves us and we actually see the Word come to life. It is then that the living Word of God becomes alive in and through the resurrected body of Christ known as His church.

JOURNAL a verse of application to strengthen any weakness that you can identify. Allow the truth of God's Word to set you free and hear that chain fall friend … hear that chain fall.

_____

_____

_____

_____

_____

_____

_____

_____

_____

_____

_____

_____

_____

_____

_____

_____

DAY 20

Locking the Doors to Temptation

"Submit yourselves, then, to God. Resist the
devil, and he will flee from you."

James 4:7 (NIV)

As an intentional disciple who is following the teachings of Jesus Christ, we are told in 2 Timothy 2:19 to turn away from wickedness. Simply put, we are to *love God* and to *hate sin*. Sometimes that is so much easier said than done. The words in 1 John 2:15 compel us, "Do not love the world [of sin that opposes God and His precepts] nor the things that are in the world" (AMP).

Don't love anything or anyone more than God. In the J.B. Phillips New Testament translation, Romans 12:2 emphasizes this toxic pressure once again: "Don't let the world around you squeeze you into its own mould, but let God re-mould your minds from within, so that you may prove in practice that the plan of God for you is good, meets all his demands and moves towards the goal of maturity." Though no follower of Christ should love the world more than God, be careful not to give into its pressure.

Loving the world too much can actually squeeze the very life out of you. This can also include worldly friends. We can be a friend to the worldly to help them find their way spiritually home, but we do not do what they do as their constant companion. Psalm 1:1-2 reinforces this principle: "Blessed is the man who walks not in the counsel of the wicked, nor stands in the way of sinners, nor sits in the seat of scoffers; but his delight is in the law of the Lord, and on His law he meditates day and night" (ESV). After all, we do grow closer with whom we spend time.

"The god of this age [Satan] has blinded the minds of unbelievers, so that they cannot see the light of the gospel of the glory of Christ, who is the image of God," reads 2 Corinthians 4:4 (NASB). Since the garden of Eden, that devious snake has been attempting to entice creation. The enemy endlessly tries to dangle whatever carrot he thinks a believer will fall for. Attempting to rob them blind, "the thief comes only to steal and kill and destroy" but the good news is that Jesus came that we "may have life, and have it abundantly" (John 10:10).

We must continue to stay vigilant to resist the desire to enter into Satan's alluring trap. The world will try to squeeze out our love for the Father to entice us to follow the world's gods. Temptations may come, but they are not from God. The devil is the tempter.

> Let no one say when he is tempted, "I am being tempted by God"; for God cannot be tempted by evil, and He Himself does not tempt anyone. But each one is tempted when he is carried away and enticed by his own lust. Then when lust has conceived, it gives birth to sin; and when sin is accomplished, it brings forth death. Do not be deceived, my beloved brethren.
> –James 1:13-16, NASB

This deception is one reason people choose to sin. They are just plain deceived and tricked by the lies of the enemy. If they had seen it coming, they would never have continued moving toward a deadly trap. However, even though no one is exempt from being tempted to sin, each one of us does have a choice. "Those controlled by the sinful nature cannot please God. You, however, are controlled not by the sinful nature but by the Spirit, if the Spirit of God lives in you…" (Romans 8:8, NIV).

Remain on the alert, for "your adversary, the devil, prowls around like a roaring lion, seeking someone to devour. But resist him, firm in your faith…" (1 Peter 5:8-9, NASB). When the enemy comes knocking on the door of your heart, do not let him come in. Be careful to not even give a foothold to the devil any more than opening the door of your home to an enemy. For once you unlock the door, he will start pushing it open. Be intentional and guard your heart by securing those gates (your ears) and windows (your eyes) so that nothing obstructs your view. Use the fruit of the Spirit called self-control to resist the temptation to even stare out the windows to see what he looks like. Do not even think about entertaining the devil; instead of inviting him in and feeding him, keep him out and starve that flesh to death.

We must fully submit ourselves to God. Let us make no allowance and no excuse for ungodly influences. "But examine everything carefully; hold fast to that which is good; abstain from every form of evil" (2 Thessalonians 5:22). With full commitment, Romans 13:14 instructs us to "make no provision for the lust of the flesh." It is like someone who is on a weight loss diet buying ice cream for the freezer just to see if it can be resisted. Besides making no sense, it is simply not practicing wisdom. Just don't buy it. When it comes to the temptations of sin, do not even make the provision. Just don't buy that lie.

Like aiming for the trash can with a paper airplane, we often miss the mark. When it comes to holiness, all of us miss the mark. By His grace and mercy, God knew that we'd wipe out before crossing the finish line, so He planned for the hand of Jesus to be there, ready to lift us up. In His goodness, God had mercy on us and sent Jesus to save us even from ourselves. "For all have sinned and fall short of the glory of God" (Romans 3:23, NASB).

It is not a sin to be tempted but it is sin when we give into it. No one is exempt from being a target. That includes Jesus. As recorded in Matthew 4:1-3, He was led into the wilderness by the Spirit to be tempted by the devil so that He could demonstrate to each one of us what to do when we *are* tempted. When the liar lied, Jesus spoke truth. As should we.

God's written Word is the weapon of our spiritual warfare and will defeat the foe every time. Speak the Word when you feel weak. Pray, even when you don't feel like praying. Pray more. "Keep watching and praying that you may *not enter* into temptation; the spirit is willing, but the flesh is *weak*," says Matthew 26:41 (NASB, emphasis added). This weakness is the very thing that makes us so vulnerable to the enemy's deceptive devices and schemes.

Faithful prayer is what strengthens your faith so you can resist temptation. Remember this: No matter what the temptation is... *love God more.*

JOURNAL a specific Scripture of truth that you feel led to stand on today.

_____

_____

_____

_____

_____

_____

_____

_____

_____

_____

_____

_____

_____

_____

_____

_____

_____

_____

_____

_____

DAY 21

Looking for Fire Escapes

"The temptations in your life are no different from what others experience. And God is faithful. He will not allow the temptation to be more than you can stand. When you are tempted, he will show you a way out so that you can endure."

1 Corinthians 10:13 (NLT)

Several years ago, the protocol for movie theaters included a verbal fire drill to precede each production. The cinema representative would actually instruct the audience in emergency preparedness before letting the movie begin. Ensuring the safety of all attendees, he or she would specifically point out each exit in the event of a fire. Purely convinced that harm could come to those who were not prepared, we listened intently. We trusted this voice of authority, certain that it was a matter of life or death.

Just as in that theater, I would like to encourage you to have a strong sense of healthy fear, one that listens to wisdom, learning to be prepared and not scared. I advise you to know the strategies of the enemy, look for the fire exits, and be prepared to run.

Remain ready to run for your life spiritually as well. We have seen that temptations are a part of living life on earth, and it is not "if" you will be tempted by the devil but "when." But the Lord will always provide us with the fire escapes if we will but look for them. In 2 Timothy 2:22, Paul tells his young son in the faith to run from youthful lusts. "Flee the evil desires of youth and pursue righteousness, faith, love and peace, along with those who call on the Lord out of a pure heart" (2 Timothy 2:22, NIV).

> No temptation [regardless of its source] has overtaken or enticed you that is not common to human experience [nor is any temptation unusual or beyond human resistance]; but God is faithful [to His word—He is compassionate and trustworthy], and He will not let you be tempted beyond your ability [to resist], but along with the temptation He [has in the past and is now and] will [always] provide the way out as well, so that you will be able to endure it [without yielding, and will overcome temptation with joy]."
>
> –1 Corinthians 10:13, AMP

God will always provide a way for each of us to escape temptation. In Matthew 4, referenced in yesterday's lesson, the Holy Spirit of God led Jesus into the wilderness on purpose. He was not sinful like us. Jesus would never have even gone down that road on His own. So why in the world did Jesus even have to walk down the road of temptation? It was *for us*. He gave us an example that we would know what to do in times of temptation. He traveled this road to leave us His footprints to follow. We must look for those steps and follow them out of the danger zone.

Please understand that even though Jesus was tempted by the devil, He was yet without sin. He really does understand the pain and struggle. "For we do not have a high priest who cannot sympathize with our weaknesses, but One who has been tempted in all things as we are, yet without sin," says Hebrews 4:15 (NASB).

Since the beginning of time in Genesis 1, Satan has used the same temptations to attempt to seduce mankind: the lust of the flesh, the lust of the eyes, and the pride of life. We find this recorded in 1 John 2:16: "For all that is in the world, the lust of the flesh and the

DAY 21

Looking for Fire Escapes

"The temptations in your life are no different from what others experience. And God is faithful. He will not allow the temptation to be more than you can stand. When you are tempted, he will show you a way out so that you can endure."

1 Corinthians 10:13 (NLT)

Several years ago, the protocol for movie theaters included a verbal fire drill to precede each production. The cinema representative would actually instruct the audience in emergency preparedness before letting the movie begin. Ensuring the safety of all attendees, he or she would specifically point out each exit in the event of a fire. Purely convinced that harm could come to those who were not prepared, we listened intently. We trusted this voice of authority, certain that it was a matter of life or death.

Just as in that theater, I would like to encourage you to have a strong sense of healthy fear, one that listens to wisdom, learning to be prepared and not scared. I advise you to know the strategies of the enemy, look for the fire exits, and be prepared to run.

Remain ready to run for your life spiritually as well. We have seen that temptations are a part of living life on earth, and it is not "if" you will be tempted by the devil but "when." But the Lord will always provide us with the fire escapes if we will but look for them. In 2 Timothy 2:22, Paul tells his young son in the faith to run from youthful lusts. "Flee the evil desires of youth and pursue righteousness, faith, love and peace, along with those who call on the Lord out of a pure heart" (2 Timothy 2:22, NIV).

> No temptation [regardless of its source] has overtaken or enticed you that is not common to human experience [nor is any temptation unusual or beyond human resistance]; but God is faithful [to His word—He is compassionate and trustworthy], and He will not let you be tempted beyond your ability [to resist], but along with the temptation He [has in the past and is now and] will [always] provide the way out as well, so that you will be able to endure it [without yielding, and will overcome temptation with joy]."
>
> –1 Corinthians 10:13, AMP

God will always provide a way for each of us to escape temptation. In Matthew 4, referenced in yesterday's lesson, the Holy Spirit of God led Jesus into the wilderness on purpose. He was not sinful like us. Jesus would never have even gone down that road on His own. So why in the world did Jesus even have to walk down the road of temptation? It was *for us*. He gave us an example that we would know what to do in times of temptation. He traveled this road to leave us His footprints to follow. We must look for those steps and follow them out of the danger zone.

Please understand that even though Jesus was tempted by the devil, He was yet without sin. He really does understand the pain and struggle. "For we do not have a high priest who cannot sympathize with our weaknesses, but One who has been tempted in all things as we are, yet without sin," says Hebrews 4:15 (NASB).

Since the beginning of time in Genesis 1, Satan has used the same temptations to attempt to seduce mankind: the lust of the flesh, the lust of the eyes, and the pride of life. We find this recorded in 1 John 2:16: "For all that is in the world, the lust of the flesh and the

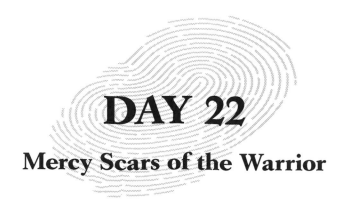

DAY 22

Mercy Scars of the Warrior

"Do not remember the sins of my youth, nor my transgressions; According to Your mercy, remember me, For Your goodness' sake, O Lord."

Psalm 25:7 (NKJV)

As I read stories recorded in the Old Testament known as the Chronicles of the Kings, I am bitterly confronted with myself. The record of actions exposed within these pages remind me that not one of us is immune to the battlefield of the enemy. From the moment that we have surrendered our hearts to the God of heaven, we are no longer of this world. There is a fierce war raging for the trophy of our soul as the enemy is out to get us to forget God's goodness. Whether fighting deep in the valleys or shouting victories on the mountaintops, we must strive to remain vigilant and to act resolutely in faithfulness to the Lord whom we serve.

One such instance is exemplified by one of the kings of Judah named Uzziah, for "... as long as he sought the Lord, God prospered him," states 2 Chronicles 26:5. However, only ten verses later we read, "Hence his fame spread afar for he was marvelously helped *until he was strong. But when he became strong, his heart was so proud that he acted corruptly, and he was unfaithful to the Lord His God*" (2 Chronicles 26:15b-16a, NASB, emphasis added).

Just as there is a fine line between compliments and conceit, there is an even finer line between confidence and pride. "The crucible is for silver and the furnace for gold, and each is tested by the praise accorded him," says Proverbs 27:21 (NASB). It is not only how well I stand under pressure that determines strength but rather how well I stand under praise. No one said that it would be easy, but keeping God as the audience of our focus will help keep us centered. When our eyes get off of Him, a trip is sure to follow. As Proverbs 16:18 says, "Pride goes before destruction, and a haughty spirit before stumbling".

Self-idolatry in an excessively proud person will eventually lead to a setback of failure. Pride is another one of those words like s-i-n that keeps "I" centered in the middle.

From the time that sin entered the world, this dismantler of thrones' one main objective was for all of us to fall. What he did not know was how jealous God is for the love of His children. When we are in the fight, our relentless God is actually on the battlefield with us! He has the scars to prove it! He is for us and not against us and He never leaves us.

"God opposes the proud but gives grace to the humble," says 1 Peter 5:5 (NASB). Though we may fall, we can stand up again once we learn to submit to His authority. No matter how long or whatever it takes, humbly or stumbling, we will learn to bow. Whether we gently choose to humble ourselves before His Majesty and willingly bend the knee or we have to tumble down into the pit we ourselves dug, we will eventually fall to our knees and "EVERY KNEE WILL BOW," declares Isaiah 45:23 (NASB, emphasis added). The beauty of this is that when we finally surrender to the Lordship of His Royal Grace, we will finally look up and see His grace extended to us.

What about you? Have you ever felt like a wounded warrior? I know that I have. As we wearily trod home after a recent battle, we begin to ache from the pain of injury. We are tired and exhausted from lifting the sword, and if no old sores are bleeding, then some new ones have appeared. When they do, it is time to clean them up and apply the balm of Gilead to heal your wounds.

All soldiers realize that they have old wounds that surface if they are on the battlefield for very long. This physical example has spiritual implications for each one of us. If the enemy cannot strike you in the present, he will try to rip off scabs from the past. Don't let him. Allow God's Love to cover spiritual pain of the past and the Great Physician Himself will heal it with His mercy.

What about the invisible wounds that only God sees? They are still there, but with time, they will start fading. As they do, keep them buried deep. Allow them to be dead in Christ. Jesus died for this, and when we do not accept His forgiveness, it is as if we have convinced our mind that the blood of Jesus was not enough. Who is on the throne then? Dear friends, if we deliberately continue sinning after we have received knowledge of the truth, there is no longer any sacrifice that will cover these sins (Hebrews 10:26).

Disciple of Jesus Christ, be intentional. Stop choosing to remember what God has chosen not only to forgive but also what God has chosen to forget. The only purpose for that scar wound now is to remind us of God's mercy (Psalm 25:7). They remain to help us remember where the blood of Jesus was applied to bring the healing we longed for.

Now is the time to allow this flesh wound to cause you a deeper appreciation for the Lord's goodness. Mercy scars reveal that you have been marked with His love and healed by His grace.

There could be a time when the Holy Spirit leads you to minister healing to another through those scars. He may use your *healed pain* to bring encouragement to others in need. Even Jesus Christ chose to keep His scars to minister resurrection hope and inspire faith in others.

> Blessed be the God and Father of our Lord Jesus Christ, the Father of mercies and God of all comfort, who comforts us in all our afflictions so that we will be able to comfort those who are in any affliction with the comfort with which we ourselves are comforted by God.
> —2 Corinthians 1:3-4, NASB

JOURNAL your desire to finally surrender the mercy scars that He knew He could trust you with, and release any open wounds to Him now that may need healing with His love.

_____

_____

_____

_____

_____

_____

_____

_____

_____

_____

_____

_____

_____

_____

_____

_____

_____

it is a spiritual posture. This solid state of position is when one *by faith is boldly standing on a promise, counting the One faithful who made the promise.* Standing spiritually still on the inside by faith demonstrates that there will be no budging until it is finished. This kind of assurance comes from confidently standing on the promises of God because He is faithful to His Word.

Strong's Concordance paints an outstanding visual for the Greek word "stillness." This type of stillness is like a surgeon who would need a patient to be still so that the Doctor may bring the wound together for healing and peace. The one who was torn into broken pieces needs to be mended before becoming whole. This is where we get the meaning for *peace* as well. Isn't that an amazing picture? Two broken pieces become one whole peace. I love that.

Please understand that God does not cause all things to happen, but as Romans 8:28 reminds us, God can cause all things to work *together* for our good. God will use whatever it takes to draw us closer to Him. He knows that peace can ultimately only be found in Him, our Prince of Peace. He desires for every painful thorn of your flesh to be taken upon Jesus at the cross for your good because He loves you. Until feelings match your healed heart, be still and stand strong upon His promises, knowing that His good is waiting for you.

JOURNAL the words to Romans 8:28. Stand on this promise by asking Jesus to cause your _ (circumstance, pain, "thing") to work out for good.

_____

_____

_____

_____

_____

_____

_____

_____

_____

_____

_____

_____

_____

_____

_____

_____

_____

_____

DAY 24

Intentional Forgiveness for Ourselves

"You, Lord, are forgiving and good, abounding in love to all who call to you. Hear my prayer, LORD; listen to my cry for mercy. When I am in distress, I call to you, because you answer me."

Psalm 86:5-7 (NIV)

No one would have thought it would be Peter to deny the Lord. No one including Peter himself. After all, not only was this fisherman of Bethsaida a friend and disciple of Jesus but also one of the 12 apostles. As he walked with Jesus daily, hearing His words and seeing His works, the only plan that Peter had premeditated was that he would live to follow Jesus. As Jesus was explaining the days that lay ahead, Peter defiantly stated that even if he had to die, never would he ever turn away. Convinced in his own mind, he spoke directly to Jesus Himself, "Even though all may fall away because of You, I will never fall away" (Matthew 26:33, NASB). Why would Peter say that? Because he never intended to fall away, and neither do we. There is a Peter in all of us.

The beautiful God that we serve knows us better than we know ourselves, so He designed a plan. "But God demonstrates His own love toward us, in that *while we were yet sinners*, Christ died for us" (Romans 5:8, NASB, emphasis added). Without God's love, there would be no forgiveness because love has absolutely everything to do with it. God has already shown us His love to us, and now it is our turn to receive it.

In every area of life, learning is a growth process. Maturing as a disciple is no exception. Forgiveness is always hard but it is especially difficult when it comes to forgiving ourselves. Releasing our own prison cell is a choice that we must make because we love God and do not want anything to separate us from drawing near to Him (Isaiah 59:2).

The following are a few forgiveness principles within Scripture that I have personally found helpful. I would strongly suggest highlighting or underlining each one in your Bible.

The Forgiveness Principle: Admit it. Quit it. Forget it.

- *Admit It:* 1 John 1:9, Psalm 32:5, Psalm 38:18

When we need forgiveness from God, we must humbly call upon God and He will give us mercy. If we have sin in our life, we need to admit it to God by confessing it to Him and asking Him for His merciful forgiveness. As we acknowledge our sin and confess it, then Psalm 32:5 and 1 John 1:9 tell us that forgiveness comes as a result: "If we confess our sins, he is faithful and just and will forgive us our sins and purify us from all unrighteousness."

- *Quit It:* Proverbs 28:13, 2 Chronicles 7:14, John 8:11

Having received God's forgiveness, we now are to stop, turn from our wicked ways, and no longer walk in the direction of our sin but completely forsake it and walk away.

- *Forget It:* Psalm 103:10-12, Philippians 3:13, Romans 4:7-8

We ask God to help us to forget even the memory that represents our past. Psalm 103:12 reassures us that God removes our sin as far as the east is from the west *from us.* Since God forgets it, with His help so can we. Psalm 66:18 cautions that if we keep regarding that iniquity or sin, then God cannot hear us.

God's "love covers a multitude of sin" (1 Peter 4:8, NASB). The blood of Jesus is more than enough and His love covers *all* of our sin. Let Him. When it comes to Peter, by receiving the forgiveness of Jesus Christ and also forgiving himself, he was able to fulfill his God-given destiny as one of the courageous leaders of the church.

Embracing God's forgiveness as a mature disciple, we too can run towards the goal and live as the apostle Paul challenges us in Philippians 3:12-15a (NIV):

> Not that I have already obtained all this, or have already arrived at my goal, but I press on to take hold of that for which Christ Jesus took hold of me. Brothers and sisters, I do not consider myself yet to have taken hold of it. But one thing I do: Forgetting what is behind and straining toward what is ahead, I press on toward the goal to win the prize for which God has called me heavenward in Christ Jesus. All of us, then, who are mature should take such a view of things.

May we steadfastly take this position and see from Jesus' point of view. Gladly join the faithful and mature who have chosen to forget the past and intentionally focus on the goal of heaven.

JOURNAL your thankfulness of God's forgiveness to you personally as you meditate on this final Scripture: "And their sins and their lawless deeds I will remember no more" (Hebrews 10:17, NASB).

_____

_____

_____

_____

_____

_____

_____

_____

_____

_____

_____

_____

_____

_____

_____

_____

_____

_____

DAY 25

Intentional Forgiveness for Others

"Forgive as the Lord forgave you."

Colossians 3:13 (NIV)

Forgiveness. It is never easy, but in the Word of God, we are told that now that we have been forgiven, we need to forgive others. Just as the Golden Rule tells us to treat others as we would want to be treated, God so generously forgives us, so we also should forgive others. That sums it up. If for no other reason, we should forgive others *because He said so.*

Extending forgiveness to those who we feel have wronged us is only possible because of God's love for us; that love is now lived out in and through us. Love, only God's love in us, is what equips us to give His grace to others. That kind of forgiveness does not come naturally but thanks be to God, it can come supernaturally by the strength which God supplies.

When the actions of others have resulted in pain for you, your response is what reveals the living proof of your changed life. As we have already seen, our love for God as a disciple is demonstrated through our obedience to Him. Our feelings have nothing to do with it and honestly, they may never change, but this is where we exercise walking by faith. Faith walks where feelings or fact do not exist. When we make a choice to walk like Jesus and determine to love like Jesus, we obey God's Word and please

Him, for "without faith, it is impossible to please God" (Hebrews 11:6, NASB).

Now let's get specific. How does God's Word tell us to confront someone who has changed the course of our life as we know it? In Matthew 18:15, we are directed that if our brother sins against us, we are to go and to show his fault to him alone, just between the two of you privately first. Verses 15-17 give us continued instructions regarding what to do if he or she does not listen to you.

Years ago, I had an instance where, after much prayer, I gently confronted someone over a painful action of the past. Rather than receiving from them my pre-conceived expectation of an apology being met, they responded completely opposite by saying, "I have no idea what you are talking about." Though this crushed me at the time, I had chosen to forgive anyway, no matter what. I could only do this with the strength that God alone had equipped me with. I had made a choice that day to walk out forgiveness… no matter what.

So what if the one you have forgiven does not respond how you hoped? *Forgive anyway.* We are responsible for our part, i.e., obedience to what God says, and not their part, i.e., how they receive it or change. Forgiveness is for *giving*, not necessarily always for receiving.

We are not to give forgiveness and grace because we are expecting something in return. Instead, we are obeying a command of God and following in the footsteps of Jesus your Lord. Ultimately, our actions are for Him.

This does not mean, however, that consequences are excused for choices made. Forgiveness is not the same thing as restored trust. It does, however, release their control over you so that the memory's power is released. Give it to God for justice, and trust Him with the outcome.

Remember Joseph in the Old Testament? He never let his circumstances get the best of him. Joseph saved his best only for God. He had a lifetime of reasons to never forgive his brothers; however, his focus was intentionally on God rather than the reasons justifying his feelings. As he waited for the opportunity to honestly deal with the truth behind the painful experiences of his past, God was still using Joseph. With loyalty, he faithfully ministered; with integrity, he served. All the while, Joseph continued to keep God as his focus. In the end, what the enemy meant for evil, God made it turn out for Joseph's good.

God can use anything broken to be restored for His glory as long as we give all the pieces to Him. Whether a victim for a day or a victim for a lifetime, the choice is yours. But I'd like to encourage you to choose freedom by not allowing forgiveness or actually unforgiveness to hold you back. Another person's actions should not suspend your present or keep you in chains for your future. Give the control key over to God. Extending His forgiveness to others results in freedom for you, so let it go, friend. It is time to forgive.

JOURNAL your desire to grow in grace by extending forgiveness to others. Pray for God's leading if there is anyone you need to speak with. If you are like me and need some specific scripture to lean into, these are a few of my favorites, Matthew 18:15-17, 21-22, 35; Mark 11:25-26; Matthew 6:12,14-15; Ephesians 4:32; Hebrews 10:12,17; and Colossians 3:13.

_____

_____

_____

_____

_____

_____

_____

_____

_____

_____

_____

_____

_____

_____

_____

_____

DAY 26

Fight the Good Fight

"Be strong in the Lord and in his mighty power."

Ephesians 6:10 (NIV)

In this world, realize that your association with Jesus Christ now identifies that you are His beloved. *His.* Oh, what a glorious word! But not everyone is happy about your new sworn allegiance. In the eyes of the adversary, you are now a marked target for the opponent to do whatever it takes to attempt to slow you down. There is a battle going on, and Satan wants to prevent you from growing and also to hurt your witness.

As a disciple of Christ, it is not a matter of *if* you will be attacked by the enemy but *when.* So how do you stand strong when facing a battle? God has given you armor to protect you and a sword to fight with. We are not using this sword against other people but against Satan.

We have already been introduced to John 10:10, which tells of the thief coming to steal, to kill, and to destroy us, but we must remember that our mighty Lord has come to give us an abundant life. He is our life-giver, protector, and defender, so we have no need to fear. God is with us.

Philippians 4:19 declares that all we need God has already met: "My God will supply all your needs according to His riches in glory in Christ Jesus" (NASB). This includes all provisions needed to withstand the enemies' schemes. We must take advantage of the protection that our God has provided for this good fight of faith. Let us examine this armor of God from Ephesians 6:10-18, which not only defines this spiritual gear, but also gives us the reason why we need it.

"[10] In conclusion, be strong in the Lord [draw your strength from Him and be empowered through your union with Him] and in the power of His [boundless] might. [11] Put on the full armor of God [for His precepts are like the splendid armor of a heavily-armed soldier], so that you may be able to [successfully] stand up against all the schemes *and* the strategies *and* the deceits of the devil. [12] For our struggle is not against flesh and blood [contending only with physical opponents], but against the rulers, against the powers, against the world forces of this [present] darkness, against the spiritual *forces* of wickedness in the heavenly (supernatural) *places*. [13] Therefore, put on the complete armor of God, so that you will be able to [successfully] resist *and* stand your ground in the evil day [of danger], and having done everything [that the crisis demands], to stand firm [in your place, fully prepared, immovable, victorious]. [14] So stand firm *and* hold your ground, HAVING TIGHTENED THE WIDE BAND OF TRUTH (personal integrity, moral courage) AROUND YOUR WAIST and HAVING PUT ON THE BREASTPLATE OF RIGHTEOUSNESS (an upright heart), [15] and having strapped on YOUR FEET THE GOSPEL OF PEACE IN PREPARATION [to face the enemy with firm-footed stability and the readiness produced by the good news].

[16] Above all, lift up the [protective] shield of faith with which you can extinguish all the flaming

arrows of the evil *one*. [17] And take THE HELMET OF SALVATION, and the sword of the Spirit, which is the Word of God. [18] With all prayer and petition pray [with specific requests] at all times [on every occasion and in every season] in the Spirit, and with this in view, stay alert with all perseverance and petition [interceding in prayer] for all God's people."

–Ephesians 6:10-18 AMP

Possessing the armor of God is not the same thing as putting it on. You must purposefully put each piece upon yourself. Does the military wait until they are being attacked on the earthly battlefield and then leave to go get their ammunition? No! Neither should we, dear friends. In the middle of the war is not the time or place to be unprepared; otherwise, the weak will soon find that they are held captive within the enemy's camp.

Spiritual soldiers must learn how to fight the good fight of faith. When our children were young, we taught them that they were young spiritual warriors. My favorite part of each morning was when we rolled up to the school. We would practice putting on the armor of God with a song that went like this: "I put on...... my helmet of salvation and my righteous breastplate, the sword of the Spirit and my shield of faith, my loins are gird with truth and my feet are shod with the preparation of peace of the word of God!" Victory cries were sure to follow with laughter.

Remember you are a child of the Living God! We are all sons and daughters of the King of Kings! So hold your head up high and know that since God is for you, He is victoriously with you. Bravely walk in the light of God's Word, carrying your shield of faith—that pleases Him. Lift high the sword of the Spirit, speaking the Word of God against the enemy. Wear your helmet of salvation upon your head to cover and protect your mind and thoughts. Stand upright before the Lord. Keep your body covered with the breast plate so that righteousness embraces your heart and shields your lungs where the Spirit of God breathes life into you. Tighten up that belt and the

Truth of God's Word will hold you up. As your feet are walking in the path of peace, be ready to spread good news.

The Bible is filled with power for this earthly journey we are on. The Name of the Lord Jesus is a strong tower but brothers and sisters, we must remember to run to it for safety. Though He is our refuge, we must relentlessly pursue Him in all of our times of trouble. Otherwise, how can He help? We must do our part.

Be alert and recognize that God is before you; God is behind you; God is beside you and it is He who is your hedge of protection. Embrace Him. He is right there with you. And when trouble comes as it does, a good soldier will realize that he is not a failure for falling down but for failing to get back up. So encourage yourself to stand up and keep marching on. "You CAN do all things through CHRIST who gives you strength," says Philippians 4:13 (emphasis added). Disciple, stand firm in this fight and know that ultimately this battle belongs to the Lord.

> "Fight the good fight of faith. Take hold of the eternal life to which you were called when you made your confession in the presence of many witnesses. In the sight of God, who gives life to everything, and of Christ Jesus."
>
> –1 Timothy 6:12-13a, NIV

JOURNAL a word of encouragement to yourself to bravely go where God leads.

_____

_____

_____

_____

_____

_____

_____

_____

_____

_____

_____

_____

_____

_____

_____

_____

_____

_____

DAY 27
Garden Friends

"A man who has friends must himself be friendly, But there is a friend who sticks closer than a brother."

Proverbs 18:24 (NKJV)

Everyone wants to celebrate with us things that are lovely... the new job, the happy birthday, the glorious wedding, the precious new baby, the adorable puppies—the "lovelies." It is easy to invite someone to join us when the beautiful flowers of life are blooming, but what about when painful thorns are all that are surrounding your broken ground of growth? Who will you ask to join you? These are what I call "Garden Friends". *

In the Old Testament, Proverbs 17:17 states, "A friend loves at all times." To be quite honest, sharing the "lovelies" comes easier for me too. Allowing a friend to love at *all times* takes laying my pride aside. Digging deeper can get downright messy and not everyone wants to be involved during suffering.

One of those "all times" surfaced for me during the lonely days of pain and hardship following the loss of my precious mother. She went home to be with the Lord after her short battle with cancer. To me, no one can take the place of my loving momma. Her life truly made a difference in mine. We were more than mother and daughter; we were friends.

No one can take the place of a loving family, and the Lord has truly blessed me more than I could ask for. But at some time in our life, we may find that in addition to our family we also need a spiritual friend that can flesh out Jesus for us. These "Garden Friends" pray for our strength—physical, mental, emotional, and spiritual. One of the hardest parts during this season was finally acknowledging that I had this need.

When those petals in that season began to fade on earth for me, I needed to have people willing to traverse hard trails alongside of me so that loneliness was not my only friend. Focusing on self too long makes one selfish; soon, it becomes easy to fall into the pit we ourselves create.

Let it be understood that I must emphasize that God must always be the very first one we run to at all times. God should always be our primary source of strength. Our family and friends are our secondary support in life. If we are going to ask someone into the garden with us, they must be able to water the seed that God first has already planted.

"My eyes shall be upon the faithful of the land, that they may dwell with me; He who walks in a blameless way is the one who will minister to me," says Psalm 101:6 (NASB). Trusted friends who walk in integrity consistently help bring out the Christ in me. By giving God's Word over their own, a "Garden Friend" continually reminds me to focus on Him even during hard times. They point me to God and His Word even when I can't seem to find Him, hear Him, or see Him—*especially* when I can't seem to find Him, hear Him, or see Him!

"Iron sharpens iron, so one man sharpens another," says Proverbs 27:17 (NASB). A friend of God can help your sword stay sharp. I need a friend who knows God so intimately that His Word will overflow from their mouth to feed me with life when I am too frail and weak to lift the spoon. These could be the times that I need their counsel and prayers most of all.

In Matthew 26:36, Jesus exposes the turmoil within those dark hours passionately as His sacrificial love is deeply demonstrated in the garden of Gethsemane. Gethsemane means "olive press" and this "pressing moment" would prove to be one of the most painful moments of Jesus' life prior to the actual crucifixion.

Proverbs 18:24 in the Message translation reminds us, "True friends will be with you through life's most soul-shaking changes." Notice that even Jesus, who was God, chose to invite a few committed, close friends into the painful moments preceding His death. If anyone on earth could have stuck it out alone, Jesus could have. However, Jesus did not choose to suffer alone during His excruciating time of struggle. Jesus took His disciples near to this area, but He chose only three—Peter, James, and John—to actually walk close with Him into the heart of the garden.

Our Lord asked them to pray, to stay alert, and to keep watch with Him while He was in sorrow and needing strength to follow the Father's will. By intentionally allowing your "Garden Friends" to join in challenging moments, they will minister to you in this fellowship of suffering.

Because our flesh is weak, we most definitely need battlefront prayer warriors willing to stay awake with us spiritually. During those long foggy nights, they can stand with us and help us to keep our eyes on Christ. They also stand for us in the gap in those trying moments when we cannot seem to hear God's voice due to spiritual, physical, and emotional exhaustion. When darkness may have clouded our view, those pure reflections of the face of Christ shine some light our way just in the nick of time. It is then that we see life from God's point of view once again.

In the wrestling matches between your heart and head where flesh and spirit struggle, our strength can be encouraged by a "Garden Friend." But remember, even on their best of days, friends are not perfect and can fall asleep on us, just like Peter, James, and John did with Jesus; after all, they are only human, but sweet Jesus, without condemnation, reminded them that "the spirit is willing but the body is weak" (Matthew 26:41, NIV).

Jesus was actually modeling for Peter, James, and John how to surrender to God's will when it is difficult. They heard the very aching of His soul as He cried out to the Father, "Not my will but

THY will be done." Jesus demonstrated for the generations to come that we must put God first and surrender our will to His. If Jesus needed to pray because He was struggling with His will versus the Father's will, shouldn't we?

If you desire "Garden Friends" and they have not arrived as of yet, do not worry but pray. God will send them your way, so pray that you recognize them when He does. Until then, be a friend to others. Pray for those in their Gethsemane to see God's presence during this, to hear God and listen to what He says and ultimately to submit to God's will with courage. Beautiful bouquets are most fragrant after the rain, so there could very well be someone crying out for you to come to their garden even now. Ask God for your heart to be sensitive to another. You may be surprised to find that you could actually be the answer to their heart's prayer and in turn find out that they could be the "Garden Friend" you who have been praying for also.

JOURNAL the names of anyone that you feel you trust to pray with you during your Gethsemanes of life and express your gratitude to them if you have not already.

_____

_____

_____

_____

_____

_____

_____

_____

_____

_____

_____

_____

_____

_____

_____

_____

_____

_____

*The term "Garden Friends" is a phrase that I respectfully use that was first coined by the late teacher-evangelist Dave Busby. This incredible man has left an indelible mark on my heart for living a life filled with passion for Christ. Dave demonstrated the importance of making every breath count during his days of victorious living with Cystic Fibrosis. Though He has gone on to heaven to be with our Lord, Dave Busby's ministry on earth continues to live on.

DAY 28
The Heart Test

"...test Me now in this," says the Lord of hosts, "if I will not open for you the windows of heaven and pour out for you a blessing until it overflows."

Malachi 3:10b (NASB)

Have you ever seen a magic trick where someone is hiding an object in one hand and you have to guess which hand it is in? Well, I have always heard that the clue is to pay close attention to the color of the magician's hands. The tightly clutched hand holding the object usually has the whiter knuckles. It sure is a good thing that God didn't ask us to prove our trust in Him with a test like that or a lot of us would have white knuckles from holding onto money too tight.

So, what is in your hand? Actually, God does not play around when it comes to trusting Him as Lord of our finances. He already knows what we are trying to keep from Him no matter how tightly we clench. The beautiful thing is that as we learn the principle of letting go, we often begin experiencing His blessings.

Psalm 50:10 says that God has all the cattle on 1,000 hills. So why does He need my money? That is just it: God does *not* need your money. He doesn't even want your money. What He wants is your heart! Tithing is just that...*a test of our heart.*

By putting God first with my money, I reverently demonstrate that God is first in my heart. If we are not tithing, we are not putting God first in our spending. If we are not careful, we may be trusting in ourselves more than God. Some people's hearts are so tightly attached to their money that it can start becoming their god without their awareness. When finances become an idol, it can be dangerous. The love of money begins to stand in the way of our approach to the throne of God and block our path to Him. Next, we become distracted, looking for the money before we can even focus on God on His throne. The unfortunate result is a slow, dangerous return to painful slavery. By withholding the tithe from God, we attempt to begin looking to ourselves rather than to God as our provider. Soon, chains of financial bondage get traded for our dance of freedom that Christ died for.

GOD must be FIRST in the heart of the intentional disciple and this also includes first in our spending. Matthew 6:21 probes, "For where your treasure is, there your heart will be also" (NIV). It is not really about treasure as much as what treasure reveals about our heart. We are to acknowledge the Lord in all our ways, including our finances: "Trust in the Lord with all your heart and lean not on your own understanding; in all your ways submit to him, and he will make your paths straight" (Proverbs 3:5-6, NIV).

This "heart test" for believers is found in Malachi chapter 3:

> "Will a man rob God? Yet you are robbing Me! But you say, 'How have we robbed You?' In tithes and offerings." You are cursed with a curse, for you are robbing Me, the whole nation of you! Bring the whole tithe into the storehouse, so that there may be food in My house, and test Me now in this," says the Lord of hosts, "if I will not open for you the windows of heaven and pour out for you a blessing until it overflows. Then I will rebuke the devourer for you, so that it will not destroy the fruits of the ground; nor will your vine in the field cast its grapes," says the Lord of hosts. "All the nations will call you blessed, for you shall be a delightful land," says the Lord of hosts.
>
> —Malachi 3:8-12 NASB

This text is the only place in the Scriptures where God tells His followers to *test Him*. The word translated "tithe" in the Bible literally means "tenth" or a "tenth part." Even more amazing is that in the Bible, the number ten represents testing. Throughout both the Old and the New Testaments, God's people have been tested multiple times. A few examples of these tens include the ten plagues in Egypt (a surrender test), the Ten Commandments (an obedience test), and the ten virgins in Matthew 25 (a preparedness test).

Specifically, the tithing principle teaches us that the first ten percent of our income is holy to the Lord. We give this ten percent tithe to our spiritual storehouse, our local church, where we are spiritually being fed, and then Jesus receives our tithes in heaven. This is what sets into motion God being able to multiply and bless the 90 percent that is left. When the first money God has given to us is the first money that we cheerfully give back to God (2 Cor. 9:7), we respectfully demonstrate that we are not owners but rather faithful stewards of that tenth; thus, we are graciously rewarded.

Tithing involves giving to God *before* you see if you're going to have enough (money, time, etc.) in your budget. Tithing demonstrates our faith in God. As we are testing God when giving our tithe, we are being tested in the area of obedience when we make the choice to tithe. By revealing our priorities, tithing declares that we are lifting up God as first place, thus initiating God's blessing on our lives. When I hear someone say that they cannot afford to tithe, the fact is they can't afford not to.

Not only does the passage in Malachi 3 state that God will bless the tither with blessings overflowing, but He also blesses the tither by rebuking the devourer for them. This is a divine hedge of protection. Yes, our God declares that He will not only bless us with provisions but also with protection!

Tithing teaches us to rely on and fear God rather than man.

> "You shall surely tithe all the produce from what
> you sow, which comes out of the field every year.
> You shall eat in the presence of the Lord, at the

place where He chooses to establish His name, the tithe of your grain, your new wine, your oil, and the firstborn of your herd and your flock, so that you may learn to fear the Lord your God always."

–Deuteronomy 14: 22-23, NASB

Please know that I understand. We all have ways that we could be tempted to spend that money from the first of our paychecks, but the first ten percent of any income scripturally belongs to God. If we keep that ten percent for ourselves, we are not giving it to God. Thus, we are taking it from God. We actually bring a curse upon ourselves because it is stolen. Let that soak in. A curse where the enemy breaks through the hedge. Do we want blessings or curses? The choice is ours.

I will conclude with this example: Pretend with me that my husband whom I love very much handed me $40 to go to the grocery store for tonight's family dinner. Imagine that I purposefully planned my grocery list to prepare an amazing meal. Meticulously, I selected each exact ingredient to meet my recipe specifications as I spent time shopping. I then arduously prepared each food to the best of my ability for those I love. I set the table, arranged the delicious foods to be served upon the table and announced that dinner was served. As the delicious aroma swirls throughout the entire house, we are both seated. However, what if I chose to give my husband a brown bag of leftovers after I ate first? How would this make him feel? Obviously not very loved. Remember, in this instance, my husband was the one who gave me the money in the first place.

In the same way, spiritual leftovers are what some of us have been giving to God. Stale crumbs at the end of a bread bag can never compare with fresh baked bread hot from the oven. Tithing is a lot like this. It is not about giving God what is left of our finances but lovingly serving Him first because He sits at the head of the table. Let us examine ourselves today and ask who we are serving first. May we always remember who is our Guest of Honor.

JOURNAL your intentional commitment to follow God in your walk of obedience with a tithe.

_____

_____

_____

_____

_____

_____

_____

_____

_____

_____

_____

_____

_____

_____

_____

_____

_____

_____

DAY 29

Intentional Aim

"Therefore, we also have as our ambition, whether
at home or absent, to be pleasing to Him."

2 Corinthians 5:9 (NASB)

My husband, Jack, is an archer. Not just the "draw back the arrow with the bow, release, let it fly and circle where it lands" kind, but the serious "focusing on a dime-sized target" kind of competitive archer. God has gifted his arms to successfully execute this skill with a strong sense of accuracy. This reward also comes as a result of many hours of practice. In fact, he is actually outside in 90 degree weather, exercising this repetitive objective as I write. My husband is what I would call "intentional." He is passionately determined to do his best and deliberately focused on his goal.

A matter of fact, all sports enthusiasts know that they have been successful when there is an actual goal or target involved to make the score. Whether the aim is focused on a net, a basket, a or bullseye really isn't that important as long as the target is *identified*. What matters is comprehending what the target actually is, positioning your body toward it, and then with determined focus, hitting it. All actions are done on purpose.

Knowing our target is essential to attain success on our field of life as well. According to the *Merriam-Webster Dictionary*, the word "aim" means "to direct a course; something one hopes or intends to accomplish." Let's make that personal. Who is directing your course? What do you hope or intend to accomplish on earth?

In 1 John 3:18-24, the apostle John teaches children of God to love one another and not to practice sin. As an intentional disciple, we are to practice doing those things that help us to mature in our faith and grow up into the likeness of Christ. Our personal aim and goal should be to please our Father God. 2 Corinthians 5:9 reveals this goal with the following words, "Therefore, we also have as our ambition, whether at home or absent, to be pleasing to Him" (NASB).

"Ambition" is also translated "goal" in the New International Version Bible. Webster continues to provide further clarity, stating that a "goal suggests something attained only by prolonged effort and hardship." That makes sense. If the objective was already achieved, there would be no challenge for growth. All meaningful growth takes time.

"Prolonged effort" implies that there is a process involved. In Psalm 78:57, the unfaithful children of Israel were well-acquainted with hardship. Unfortunately, they wandered aimlessly without following God's goal for them. The King James Version says that they "turned aside like a deceitful bow," rather than hitting the mark with straight arrows or, as the Living Bible paraphrases, "like a crooked arrow, they missed the target of God's will." This passage confirms that the children of Israel not only missed the mark, but they also wandered around in circles. They were distracted as they kept turning back. It is anonymously said that "God allowed the children of Israel to wander in the wilderness for 40 years not just to get them out of Egypt but also to get the Egypt out of them". How sad but true.

Ultimately, they were prepared and ready to draw near to His presence but only after much suffering and hardship. Once they removed themselves from their central focus, they began to clearly see God again. Then they were able to whole-heartedly worship the God their hearts longed for.

Accomplishing human goals should never outweigh our

obedience in focusing on the target of God's will. In Romans 8:8, we are reminded that "those who are in the flesh [sinful nature] cannot please God." Our aim should always be to please God first but how do we know what will please Him? Simply put, by living according to His Word. 2 Timothy 3:16 adds further clarity, "All Scripture is inspired by God and is useful to teach us what is true and to make us realize what is wrong in our lives. It corrects us when we are wrong and teaches us to do what is right" (NLT). As we learn what God's Word says we are more likely to walk it out.

We can also learn what will please God by intentionally praying and asking Him to give wisdom according to His Word. Once we ask in our prayer of faith, we listen for Him. It is then that He may quietly speak to us within our own spirit by the voice of the Holy Spirit living inside of you. There may be instances when His direction is given through a song or a meaningful sermon. The Lord may also give guidance through the counsel of other mature believers. This is scriptural. Do know that when He uses someone to speak advice through, God's Word and His Will always agree leaving a peaceful confirmation and witness within you.

By choosing to intentionally aim to please God, your focus and determination will help eliminate distractions and build faithfulness in your journey "so that you will walk in a manner worthy of the Lord, *to please Him* in all respects, bearing fruit in every good work and increasing in the knowledge of God" (Colossians 1:10, NASB).

JOURNAL three personal goals that you can identify that please God. Pray that the Lord will help you to remain disciplined so as not to wander aimlessly but rather to remain pleasing unto Him.

_____

_____

_____

_____

_____

_____

_____

_____

_____

_____

_____

_____

_____

_____

_____

_____

_____

_____

DAY 30

Worry Not. Fear Not.

"I sought the Lord, and He answered me and
delivered me from all my fears."

Psalm 34:4 (NASB)

Following fear leads nowhere. As I type these words, our world is desperately struggling with the COVID-19 global pandemic. The daily count of positive cases has now reached millions worldwide with many ending in death. A vaccine is constantly in the process of being created to save lives. We are crying out to God for the healing of our nation both spiritually and physically. Our prayers matter because this danger is real. Many people that do not know Christ have only a grave outlook. They are literally scared to death as they allow their hope to be stolen. When hope is missing, then fear (real or imagined) can take over and lead to more worry which can lead to more fear, resulting in a downward spiral. But remember, following fear leads nowhere.

So rather than being scared, our nation is continually being encouraged to stay prepared. Across our nation, we have been in "safe mode" with home sheltering to prevent the spread, the implementation of six feet of social distance, and protective face masks becoming the norm due to the high risk of contagion. Using wisdom and remaining alert still raise concerns but concern is not the same thing as worry.

Whatever we focus on seems to expand, even when it comes through the nightly news. Worry will not change our circumstances, but unfortunately worrying changes *us*. Romans 10:17 reveals that our faith (in anything) comes by hearing and hearing (and hearing and hearing). Soon we believe what we hear if it is repeated long enough and despite whether it is true or not. But thankfully, during this season, believers from around the world are fervently praying that many lives will be saved as God uses this pandemic for many to come to know Him in the midst of this.

One thing that I have noticed is that as people are learning to cope during this quarantine, many are practicing mindfulness. But being mindful is never the same as being mindfully aware of God. Even in times when there is no pandemic, God's voice still needs to be the loudest voice we listen to. Our faith must be greater than all our fear. Romans 10:17 does not end with "Faith comes by hearing, and hearing," but it continues, "Faith comes by hearing, and hearing *by the word of God*" (emphasis added). When we spend time in the Scriptures, the truth is magnified. This helps us to see God as bigger than the circumstance. As our faith increases, our worry decreases; as we trust God more, we fear less.

In Joshua 1, the Lord tells Joshua to meditate on His Word day and night in order for him to have good success. The good news continues in verse 9: "Have I not commanded you? Be strong and courageous! Do not tremble or be dismayed, for the Lord your God is with you wherever you go" (Joshua 1:9, NASB).

I must confess that though I have memorized this verse, I still wrestle with the temptation to fear at times. Part of the problem has been that in the past when navigating uncharted waters, I would struggle with being in control. But why? What I have found is that when I am not in control, I sometimes forget that He is with me, and I am tempted to worry. All because of fear.

Which is exactly the time to turn up the volume of God's voice because fear is a liar and we do not have to listen to it. Psalm 34:4 reminds us that the Lord is our deliverer from all fear. He surrounds us with songs of deliverance both day and night. Our precious Lord comforts us even when we don't know it (Psalm 32:7). And it is this perfect love of God that can actually cast out our fear. He wants to get rid of it. Knowing that we would need reminding, He actually placed the words "fear not" within the pages of Scripture 365 times. That is one for each of our 365 days in a year!

I have been given ample opportunities to apply those "fear nots" in my life. Psalm 34:4 and 7 are one example: "I sought the Lord, and He answered me and delivered me from all my fears. ... The angel of the Lord encamps around those who fear Him, and rescues them." This verse became real to me one day as faith-in-action was given a front row seat one September afternoon in my car.

I was confronted face-to-face with a near-death experience when I was T-boned by a speeding car. All air bags deployed, my eyeglasses went one way, my cell phone another, and in the moments leading up to what I thought would be my last on earth, a precious angel of a lady pressed her head into the car fearlessly and asked who she could call. Thankfully, I remembered my husband's phone number. She then stepped away to notify him. I was alone but I wasn't.

Sounds of ambulances and unknown voices surrounded me, and within seconds, my world went dark. I could not see anything and I felt as if I was underwater. I was alone but I wasn't. I was certain that these were my last heartbeats on earth, and I can say with full honesty I had no fear. I was embraced in peace. I was alone but I wasn't. With Jesus as Savior and Lord of my life, I undeniably knew that I would be with Him in heaven within moments.

During those precious silent moments in the dark, it was just He and I, so I prayed within my heart. "Lord, may You be glorified even in this." I told God that if He chose for me to live, I would continue to strive to serve Him to the best of my ability, even if I would be serving Him blind. Then all of a sudden, I heard the sound of my sweet husband's voice comforting me: "Sherry, I'm here." I said, "Jack, I can't see anything." With strength in his words, Jack said, "It's okay. I am not going anywhere. I will never leave you." He never did.

My amazing husband's sacrificial, unending love was

demonstrated far beyond what I could have imagined during that season of recovery as weeks turned into many months. My servant-hearted, compassionate daughter and kind son surrounded me with never-ending love as they ministered to me as they would have served their Jesus. I never knew that I could possibly love them any more than I already did, but I was wrong. More than my children, they were friends. They now had become "Garden Friends". More than I could have ever imagined, allowing my family to care for my needs was difficult but I had no choice. I needed them. I guess it was time for my pride to lay down, even though it wanted to remain in control.

Tears are streaming down my face as I recount this because that event was a defining moment for my future. Honestly, if it had not occurred, I do not know if I would have actually given myself permission to write down the pages within this book. For too many years, too many excuses stood in my way of obedience. I can relate to Martin Luther when he said, "How soon not now becomes forever."

It was also through this experience that God taught me something spiritually powerful about His presence with me. It was through those lonely times when "I was alone but I wasn't" that I finally saw that God was there. He really, really never left me. Now I know that my fear of fear changed that day and I can honestly say that my healthy fear of God outweighs my unhealthy fear of man. My fear of God also outweighs my fear of failure, my fear of success, and even my fear of change. It may have taken a near-death experience for me to really fearlessly start to live the life God designed me for.

A good life at the sacrifice of God's best is not worth settling for. Acknowledging His presence with us in every circumstance will inspire our confidence to bravely walk where God leads. So, friend, worry not and fear not. It is in knowing that God is with us that we can courageously say, *"I have no fear in death; therefore, I should have no fear in life."*

JOURNAL one of the following faith-filled verses with a personal application. By substituting your specific concern within God's promise, it will help you be fearless when you are tempted to worry.

_____

_____

_____

_____

_____

_____

_____

_____

_____

_____

_____

_____

Psalm 56:3: "When I am afraid, I will put my trust in You."

Deuteronomy 31:6, 8: "Be strong and courageous, do not be afraid or tremble at them, for the Lord your God is the one who goes with you. He will not fail you or forsake you. ... The Lord is the one who goes ahead of you; He will be with you. He will not fail you or forsake you. Do not fear or be dismayed."

DAY 31
Your God Story

"You are our letter, written in our hearts, known and read by all
men; being manifested that you are a letter of Christ, cared for
by us, written not with ink but with the Spirit of the living God,
not on tablets of stone but on tablets of human hearts."

2 Corinthians 3:2 (NASB)

Everyone has a story. There are some people that can be read like a
book while others remain more difficult. What we do know is that
others take notice. In today's verse, the apostle Paul reminds the
church in Corinth of the value of their God story or, rather, the value
of their God in their story.

Once we have accepted Jesus to be our Lord and Savior, He is the
supreme authority to our every decision. Rather than one's career or
position of leadership, it is the presence of God within us that really
defines who we are. It is your Jesus.

The size and shape of the character of Christ in our lives is daily
being chiseled from our once stony hearts so that the world can
discover Him for themselves. Our daily lives either attract others
to Him or distract others from seeing Him. This is because our life
is a living testimony filled with proof of all that God has written
upon our hearts. Louder than words, the echo of our actions may
last longer than our lifetime because the Jesus seen in us will outlive
our physical lives on earth.

How you choose to use your life matters not only to God but also to generations of people to come. Those who have walked their journey of faith before us left a lasting legacy for us to follow, and you are doing the same for the next generations: "For whatever was written in earlier times was written for our instruction, so that through perseverance and the encouragement of the Scriptures we might have hope" (Romans 15:4, NASB).

Just as God spoke the world into existence, know that God spoke you into life as well. And God's words are not empty words but ones that are filled with resurrection life power. Know that God will accomplish what His Word says. These are action words that are living, so you need to continue to keep His spoken Word alive in you.

There are over 700 promises of God in His Word for you to immerse yourself in. Knowing how God sees you will enlighten your view as your pages are written. Take time to read what God says about you. Read it aloud to yourself and just listen. By hearing His Word, your faith will grow to believe that you truly are who He says that you are. *You are His.*

Receive what the precious blood of Christ speaks over you and embrace the hope of God's will for your life as you seek the good future He has planned. "'For I know the plans I have for you,' says the Lord. 'They are plans for good and not for disaster, to give you a future and a hope'" (Jeremiah 29:11, NLT).

Rather than learning this lesson at the finish line, let us realize that though God has a race marked out for us, our purpose all along was really His. God is not a part of our life plan; rather, we are a part of His. He is not just in our story of life but He has graciously allowed us to participate in His story. This life is all about Him, His plans, and His purposes. Therefore, may He continually be the love of our life and the true desire of our hearts. "Yes, Lord, walking in the way of your laws, we wait for you; your name and renown are the desire of our hearts" (Isaiah 26:8, NIV).

Pondering how to close, I humbly want to thank you for allowing me to share these days of devotion with you. My prayer is that your path with Christ will continue to flourish as you grow stronger in respect of your salvation. As sons and daughters of the King of Kings, may you embrace all that He has for you as His will is done on earth as it is in heaven. For God is not the footnote commentary, but the actual Author of the book of your life. He is the Alpha and Omega, the Beginning and the End, the A to the Z of His every letter of His every Word. He is the Author and the Finisher of your faith, and He has written the greatest love story ever told... *for you.* I encourage you to let the world read the chapters in your life so they can see His story in yours. For He is your once upon a time and He will be your happily ever after as you live eternally with Him as a disciple of Jesus Christ.

JOURNAL a specific action step that you will intentionally take beginning tomorrow during your quiet time to continue growing as a mature disciple of Jesus Christ.

_____

_____

_____

_____

_____

_____

_____

_____

_____

_____

_____

_____

_____

_____

_____

_____

_____

_____

_____

PRAYERS:

_____

_____

_____

_____

_____

_____

_____

_____

_____

_____

_____

_____

_____

_____

_____

_____

_____

_____

PRAISES:

_____

_____

_____

_____

_____

_____

_____

_____

_____

_____

_____

_____

_____

_____

_____

_____

_____

_____

PRAYERS:

_____

_____

_____

_____

_____

_____

_____

_____

_____

_____

_____

_____

_____

_____

_____

_____

_____

_____

_____

_____

PRAISES:

_____

_____

_____

_____

_____

_____

_____

_____

_____

_____

_____

_____

_____

_____

_____

_____

_____

_____

About the Author

Sherry Dale passionately encourages all believers to follow the prompting of I Peter 2:2,3 (NASB) and "grow in respect to salvation, if you have tasted the kindness of the Lord." She considers this book a spiritual call to action for all disciples of Jesus Christ to purposefully obey Matthew 28:20 by not only learning what Jesus says but sharing it with others.

What began as a small Freshmen girls' bible study from a college dorm room in Mississippi has continued to grow. Whether in small groups or large group gatherings, compelled to teach others how to follow God's Word, Sherry strives to help all ages apply it to everyday life.

As a minister's wife for over 38 years, Sherry sincerely appreciates the journey that God has led them on. Whether inside the church or outside the church, she realizes that though mission field locations may change, His mission never does. For the past 17 years, she has been serving and loving God's youth as a middle school teacher.

When Sherry is not teaching, writing or enjoying her happy place at home, she can be found within the community at one of her pop-up booths. As founder of Missionary Marketplace, she actively supports the empowerment of women and children at risk of trafficking by providing a market for local and global missionary artisans. Sherry and her husband Jack enjoy living in beautiful Tennessee, where they are blessed to have two grown children, Summer and Jackson.

Printed in the United States
By Bookmasters